Prepared Interviewing for Educators

This book will help you interview successfully for your first job—or a new role—in education. Author Scott Lempka offers simple, chronological steps to help you prepare for your interview and show yourself in the best possible light. Topics include:

♦ Researching job opportunities

♦ Using the Big Five strategy to showcase your achievements

♦ Building Example Sandwiches to illustrate your experience

♦ Following an Interview Countdown to prepare for your interview

♦ Practicing sample interview questions in a variety of categories

In addition, this updated edition includes new information on networking through social media. With the tools and expert advice in this book, you'll be able to anticipate what your educational employers desire, and you'll gain the confidence you need to land your dream job.

Scott Lempka is a nationally recognized school leader with 20 years' experience as a teacher, instructional coach, and administrator. Scott currently serves as principal of Parker Elementary School in Elk River, Minnesota.

Also Available from Routledge Eye On Education

(www.routledge.com/K-12)

Your First Year:

How to Survive and Thrive as a New Teacher
Todd Whitaker, Katherine Whitaker, Madeline Whitaker Good

Classroom Management from the Ground Up
Todd Whitaker, Katherine Whitaker, Madeline Whitaker Good

What Great Teachers Do Differently, 2nd Edition:
17 Things That Matter Most
Passionate Learners, 2nd Edition:
How to Engage and Empower Your Students
Pernille Ripp

Rigor and Assessment in the Classroom
Barbara R. Blackburn

101 Answers for New Teachers and Their Mentors,
3rd Edition:
Effective Teaching Tips for Daily Classroom Use
Annette Breaux

Motivating Struggling Learners:
10 Ways to Build Student Success
Barbara R. Blackburn

Rigor and Differentiation in the Classroom: Tools
and Strategies
Barbara R. Blackburn

Prepared Interviewing for Educators

A Guide for Seeking Employment

Second Edition

Scott Lempka

Routledge
Taylor & Francis Group

NEW YORK AND LONDON

Second edition published 2019
by Routledge
52 Vanderbilt Avenue, New York, NY 10017

and by Routledge
2 Park Square, Milton Park, Abingdon, Oxon, OX14 4RN

Routledge is an imprint of the Taylor & Francis Group, an informa business

First edition published by Pilgrim Point Publishing 2017

Library of Congress Cataloging-in-Publication Data
Names: Lempka, Scott, author.
Title: Prepared interviewing for educators : a guide for seeking employment / Scott Lempka.
Description: Second edition. | New York : Routledge, 2019. | Includes bibliographical references.
Identifiers: LCCN 2018058827 (print) | LCCN 2019007503 (ebook) | ISBN 9780429199257 (ebook) | ISBN 9780367189266 (hbk) | ISBN 9780367189273 (pbk) | ISBN 9780429199257 (ebk)
Subjects: LCSH: Teachers–Employment–United States. | Teaching–Vocational guidance–United States | Employment interviewing–United States.
Classification: LCC LB1780 (ebook) | LCC LB1780 .L46 2019 (print) | DDC 371.1023–dc23
LC record available at https://lccn.loc.gov/2018058827

ISBN: 978-0-367-18926-6 (hbk)
ISBN: 978-0-367-18927-3 (pbk)
ISBN: 978-0-429-19925-7 (ebk)

Typeset in Palatino
by Swales & Willis, Exeter, Devon, UK

Visit the eResources: www.routledge.com/9780367189273

For my wife, Kari, and our children, Charlotte, Dean, and Rosemary.

Contents

Introduction

Consider for a moment the amount of time you have invested in preparing for a career in education. Perhaps you sought an associate's degree. You may have completed a four- or five-year college program to be a teacher, counselor, or school social worker. Others among you have spent years of postgraduate study in the field. Regardless of your professional path, you have invested years of your time. Now one daunting thing stands between you and your desired position: the interview.

In an interview lasting thirty to forty-five minutes, employers will form countless opinions about you, your skills, social aptitude, professionalism, and ultimately your ability to further the success of their school. Consider how important interviewing is to realizing a person's professional dreams: you might think candidates would put hours into preparing for this moment so they could go into the interview ready to clearly articulate the skills that will make them a significant asset to their prospective employer.

To Prepare or Not?

Unfortunately, I can say from personal experience that this is seldom the case. As a school administrator who has conducted hundreds of interviews, I find that in most cases, candidates arrive at the interview woefully unprepared, which leaves them at the mercy of the interview committee. If the "right" questions are asked (the questions

As a school administrator who has conducted hundreds of interviews, I find that in most cases, candidates arrive at the interview woefully unprepared, which leaves them at the mercy of the interview committee.

the candidate is ready to answer), the interview can go well. However, if the committee is looking for anecdotal examples or asking questions that delve into job-related areas that the candidate has not considered, the interview becomes a painful process punctuated by long pauses and shallow, nervous answers.

Surprisingly, despite the importance of the interview session to landing a desired position, relatively little research or commentary is available on the topic. We do know that many preparatory programs do not include any required interview training. In fact, some experts suggest that, because many candidates feel intimidated or inadequate, those feelings actually reduce the likelihood that they will prepare or practice for important interview opportunities (Miller et al., 2014). I have heard candidates state prior to an interview that they are not going to practice or prepare, because they want to be fresh or they do not want to seem rehearsed. Although seeming overly rehearsed in the interview is certainly not a desired outcome, neither is being uncomfortably or nervously unprepared. Put simply, prepared interviewing is becoming a lost art. Or taking another view, I could argue that it is a nonexistent art, the importance of which has yet to be fully realized!

Jobs are won and lost in the interview room. A number of years ago I interviewed a candidate for a teaching position for which he was very well qualified. Two questions into the interview, he had it in the bag. He had responded with detailed, yet concise answers that were insightful and demonstrated his relevant experience. Then the wheels came off. With each subsequent question, he began to lose confidence, and his answers became longer. It was as though he felt the need to expound upon each answer to include every possible idea or thought for which the committee members could be looking. As interviewers, we were straining to ask the next question, but we couldn't get a word in edgewise. The result? An interview that ultimately had to be called for time and a candidate still looking for a job. To this day, I wonder if he ever knew how close he was to landing that position— if he had simply prepared an interview plan and stuck to it!

On the flip side, I have interviewed candidates who came to the interview with less experience than others in the interview pool, but who were able to articulate their platform for hire clearly and with confidence. In these cases, the committee members walked away saying, "This is someone I want to work with!"

Why Would You Leave It to Chance?

If you have ever selected a college, been married, gone on a trip out of town, or bought or sold a property, you no doubt put time into preparation. You did your homework. You researched which schools had your desired degree program and what the cost would be. Perhaps you determined who could provide the best wedding cake for the price. You contacted a realtor and studied the market to determine how much house you could afford or which neighborhoods have the best schools. Planning for a trip, you probably spent time reviewing maps, planning places to stop. You looked for attractions and restaurants to visit along the way. What you didn't do is leave the education, wedding, trip, or major purchase to chance. You didn't say, "I want to let what happens happen," and leave the outcome to fate. Why should interviewing for a key professional opportunity be any different? When faced with the opportunity to take hold of the job of your dreams, why would you leave anything to chance?

> **When faced with the opportunity to take hold of the job of your dreams, why would you leave anything to chance?**

In twenty years of being interviewed and interviewing candidates, I've seen it all. I've seen great successes and abysmal failures. I've long been fascinated by the interview process and have taken careful stock of the techniques and strategies that have led to professional successes. I've also observed behaviors and approaches that have consistently resulted in failure. In the course of my own career in education, I have been interviewed numerous times and have a hire-rate of more than 90 percent.

This is not to say that my interview experience has been failure-free. Early in my professional career, I walked away from a thirty-minute interview with fifteen minutes to spare and spent the entire ride home thinking about what I should have said but didn't think to.

I have analyzed each of my successes and failures, and those of the candidates I have interviewed, and I have synthesized them into a proven formula that works. These skills have now been compiled into this book. In addition to the instruction in each chapter, I've provided sample interview questions, checklists, and worksheets to help you navigate through this process. (These tools are also available in a larger size that you can download from www.routledge.com/9780367189273.) Everything you need to accomplish a rock star interview is right here in your hands.

The goal of this book is to provide a framework that will prepare you to be a polished and confident interviewee in an education-related job interview. Although many of the examples contained in these pages focus on teachers, the precepts I teach easily translate to school counselors, psychologists, and social workers. Barriers to success such as nervousness, difficulty speaking publicly, or even lack of experience can be overcome with a reasonably small amount of preparation.

This book is also designed to be a life-long companion during your professional journey. Few teachers, counselors, etc. will remain in the same position during their entire career. Most will desire to apply for new opportunities as they present themselves. Some may choose to pursue leadership or administrative positions as their career progresses. This book provides a proven formula that can be successfully applied to any educational opportunity.

Not surprisingly, most principals enter the interview process with a pretty good idea of the candidate qualities for which they are looking. This book will help you to anticipate what qualities educational employers desire and prepare you to walk out of the interview knowing you expressed everything you had intended and presented yourself in the best possible light. You will learn to see the interview through the eyes of the interview committee. In short, I will teach you my proven method for prepared interviewing!

About the Author

 **Scott Lempka** is a nationally recognized school leader with 20 years of experience as a teacher, instructional coach, and administrator. Scott currently serves as principal of Parker Elementary School in Elk River, Minnesota. During his time as a principal in the Anoka-Hennepin and Elk River Area School Districts, Scott's schools have consistently been recognized for high performance by the Minnesota Department of Education. In 2016, Parker Elementary won the U.S. Department of Education Blue Ribbon Schools Award after ranking third overall in the state for reading proficiency. Scott earned his bachelor's degree in elementary education and psychology from Gustavus Adolphus College in St. Peter, Minnesota, and his master's degree in curriculum and instruction from Eastern Washington University in Cheney, Washington. He is a member of the Minnesota Elementary School Principals' Association. Scott and his wife, Kari, have three children.

eResources

As you read this book, you'll notice the eResources icon next to the following tools. The icon indicates that these tools are available as free downloads on our website, www.routledge.com/ 9780367189273, so you can easily print them to use or distribute.

1

Do Some Recon

When it comes to landing a position with your desired school or organization, the importance of the interview is firmly established. The good news is that you can follow a few simple steps to ensure you are prepared to present yourself to your prospective employer in the best possible light during an interview. In this chapter, we will focus on (1) ways to discover what a school or district wants and needs and (2) ways to network with those who have the power to push your résumé from the circular file to the interview pile.

Do Your Research

School administrators go into the interview session with a picture in mind of the kind of candidate they want to hire based on the needs of their building. Perhaps they are looking for someone with experience teaching in the primary grades or providing reading interventions.

Maybe they want someone with a reading or mathematics license endorsement. They may be looking for a school social worker with a background in the mental health field or extensive experience teaching self-regulation strategies.

Sometimes these desired new-hire qualities are known only to the interview committee and impossible for the candidate to determine. In most cases, however, a candidate willing to do a little detective work can go into the interview with a pretty good idea of what the interview team wants.

As an example, early in my career, I was a substitute teacher seeking a permanent position in my local public school district. Each time I substituted in one of the district's schools, I spent time familiarizing myself with the curriculum. When a fourth-grade position opened in one of the buildings where I had previously worked, I went to the staff members I knew and asked questions about the initiatives that were of particular focus in the building. I also inquired about the principal and what she valued in a teacher. At the time, "No Child Left Behind" legislation was new and statewide testing was becoming a big reality. Through the relationships I had developed in the building, I became aware that the committee was focused on finding someone who was familiar with the state's new academic standards. I also found out that the principal was concerned with student behavior and wanted someone with strong classroom-management skills.

Prior to the interview, I located a copy of the state academic standards and brushed up on them. I also spent time rehearsing my philosophy regarding student discipline and classroom management. Finally, I worked on coming up with examples of times when I had put my disciplinary philosophy to successful use with students.

When I was called in for the interview, I nervously walked into the room, shook the interview committee members' hands, and sat right down in the principal's chair. I could have died when she calmly and flatly noted that I was in her seat and would need to move. When the questions started, however, I found that I had already thought through many of the topics they were asking me to speak about. As a result, I had many examples and ideas on the tip of my tongue. When the smoke cleared, I had my first public school teaching job.

The point of this story is that this interview experience taught me a valuable lesson: a little preparation can go a long way and may even overcome other shortcomings like accidentally sitting in the boss's chair!

In the digital age, there is an ever-growing number of places to go for fresh, relevant information about schools and school districts. A quick search of online local newspaper archives will tell you the hot topics facing the district, recent awards won, and even curricular focuses. Most state departments of education have online tools that not only provide recent data on school performance and demographics, but in many cases provide grades indicating strengths and areas for improvement within schools.

While you're deciding to which districts or organizations you would like to apply, it is a good idea to search the organization's website for information about the process for becoming a continuing contract or tenured employee. Many school districts will also post the master agreements, including salary schedules, for each of their bargaining groups to the district's website.

Most schools and principals are now connected to social media, making tools like LinkedIn, Twitter, and Facebook sites easy places to learn more about the professional passions and expertise of those who might be conducting your interview. A little time spent browsing these online resources can unlock key information and even help you avoid potential interviewing landmines.

As you research, keep a notebook or file to record your findings. This can be a great place to include questions that come up as you research. There is typically a time at the end of the interview for you to ask a couple of questions. Writing a few good questions that come up during your research can save you a step later.

Every school has professional development topics that are of particular focus. For some schools, it is using technology to create flipped classrooms. It might be the implementation of guided reading strategies or differentiated instructional strategies. With a little networking and research, a candidate can easily learn a school's focus and spend time researching the topic prior to the interview. However, be careful here!

Buzzwords and catch phrases can get you in trouble if you are not prepared to prove you have experience with them.

As an administrator, I have experienced this foible in interviews. For example, in recent years, the practice of differentiating instruction to meet the varying needs of learners has been a big topic in schools. "Differentiation" has become a buzzword that has echoed up and down the halls of almost every school in the nation. This being the case, during interviews, I often hear candidates share how differentiation is a big part of their teaching. They say such things as, "I like to use differentiation in my classroom." When asked, however, for examples of how they do this, many candidates struggle. Catch phrases will do you no good if you can't provide concrete examples of how you have carried out the concepts in your professional practice. For any buzzword you plan to throw out during the interview session, be prepared to provide an example of how you have used the strategy or concept in a productive way with students.

If you are applying for your first job in education, you may be thinking, "But I have no professional experience!" Relax! You have spent months completing student teaching, practicum and/or intern- ship experiences. These *are* professional experiences. And when examples are needed, you can draw upon them during the interview.

Network, Network, Network

If you want a job bad enough, you will spend time researching the schools and districts to which you are applying. Every school has needs, wants, and fiscal responsibilities that determine the types of employees for which they are looking. Keep your ear to the rail.

Network to learn the buzzwords in your field. Use social media, such as LinkedIn, Twitter, and other platforms, to follow people who are on the cutting edge of your educational specialty. Attend conferences and, if possible, become a member of professional organizations within the field of education. Often these organizations have intern- or student-level memberships that can provide you access to relevant trainings, conferences, and networking opportunities at a fraction of the price that full members pay.

The bottom line is that *whom* you know can be as important as *what* you know.

The bottom line is that *whom* you know can be as important as *what* you know. Take time to network, because I promise you, your prospective employer is.

Think about it. For the average teaching position, there may be from fifty to more than a hundred candidates. When the candidate pool is large, districts do not have time to waste interviewing teaching, counselling, social work, or other candidates who look good on paper but don't really measure up in real life. For this reason, principals and district administrators are constantly networking with each other. As a public school administrator, I can't count how many times I have been asked, "When you interviewed last week, did you have any candidates who looked really strong?" When supervisors have a temporary employee who has served their school or organization well, they let others within the district know. Sometimes they will even share this information with others they trust who work outside of their district. Likewise, when someone creates drama, struggles with punctuality, or causes stress within the organization, this news makes its way around as well.

The point I am making here is that you need to make the most of every opportunity. Whether in an internship, a temporary teaching position, or even a chance encounter with a principal, teacher, or curriculum director at the grocery store, leverage every opportunity to leave a good impression and make a name for yourself with those who might later be viewing your application.

Interviewing—Always!

Once I had a friend who was being considered for a position operating a store for a major fast food chain. She was asked if she would like to help a local restaurant branch that was sponsoring a fun run event. Sensing an opportunity to network, she eagerly accepted. At the event, she handed out water and food and had many conversations with a number of restaurant operators from the region. She even had a conversation with one of the corporate bigwigs who was in town to support the event. At the end of the day, while cleaning up, one of the local restaurant operators asked her how it went. She smiled and said that it had been fun. He then said, "You know you were being interviewed, right?" My friend paused, a little confused. He went on to say that this particular restaurant giant uses every possible interaction to size up their candidates. Gulp!

Professional circles within the field of education are no different.

The key message here is that you are always being interviewed. It doesn't matter whether you are talking to the secretary in the main office or a teacher you ran into at your child's soccer game. When you are in the presence of people who work in the field of education, you are always being interviewed.

> **It doesn't matter whether you are talking to the secretary in the main office or a teacher you ran into at your child's soccer game. When you are in the presence of people who work in the field of education, you are always being interviewed.**

Networking While You "Test-Drive"

If you are fortunate enough to finish your degree and be hired directly out of a college or preparatory program, good for you! For many educators, however, there will be a period of time spent substitute teaching or filling in for a long-term absence. This isn't a bad thing! Teaching as a substitute allows you to test-drive many different class- rooms, classroom management plans, and curriculums. It also gives you a daily opportunity to network with teachers and principals in a variety of different buildings. Get these people to know and appreciate your work and you will be getting calls to interview when a position comes open.

I have heard teaching candidates say things like, "You don't want to become too valuable as a substitute, because schools will want to keep you available as a sub, so will not hire you." Nothing could be further from the truth. When permanent teaching and other positions become available within a school, principals want the most qualified and effective person possible in the position. Substitute teaching allows principals to test-drive your skills in a temporary capacity. Think about it. Principals know that if you are this good as a substitute in their school, if they don't hire you full-time, some other school is surely going to snatch you up. If you prove you are too good to miss, you will be called when it is time to interview—no matter how valuable you are on the substitute list.

Seizing Golden Opportunities

I once knew a substitute teacher who experienced this first-hand. One day, after spending the afternoon teaching in a fifth grade classroom, he dismissed his students and found that he had about twenty minutes of duty time left and nothing to do. Rather than leave early or read a book, as many other substitutes often did, he decided to walk down to the media center and ask the media teacher if he could help her with anything. At first she stared at him as though he were nuts, but eventually, she said, "I always have books to shelve. You could help with that."

So he spent about half an hour shelving books and talking to the teacher before gathering his things and heading home. During that time, he found out they were both originally from the same place. They bantered a little about favorite places they visited growing up … small talk. Months later, he was hired to work full-time in that building as a fourth-grade teacher. The secretary later confided in him that he did more good for himself that day than he realized. Apparently, the principal had had an ongoing frustration that substitute teachers almost always left as soon as their students were dismissed. No one had ever asked to help with menial tasks, such as shelving books. Without realizing it, he had made himself stand out in the crowd. That is half the battle.

The same goes for student teaching and practicum experiences required by your university or teacher preparatory program. Rather than viewing these requirements as a hoop you have to jump through, seize them as a golden opportunity to network and meet influential people within a school district. I can't count how many times I have seen positive experiences within a candidate's student teaching, practicum, or internship experience that led to numerous free references to administrators about an up-and-coming educator who is "too good to miss."

Know the Mission and Vision

Often schools and school districts will list their vision or mission statement on their website—or even on the walls of the school. Become familiar with this. And be prepared to give examples of how your philosophy and work experiences have demonstrated the beliefs and ideals upon which the school's mission is built. For example, let's say the mission statement of the school you are applying to is this: "We are committed to preparing students to be respectful and responsible lifelong learners." Make sure you enter the interview with examples that demonstrate how you incorporate respect and responsibility into your classroom culture. Leave the employer feeling that this is a part of who you are and how you approach your craft, and you will go a long way toward earning a job.

Scrub Your Social Media

If you are chosen for an interview, you have survived the first and biggest cut. Districts receive tens, hundreds, even thousands of applications. Receiving an invitation to interview means that you have survived the initial screening process. This is good news. Take a moment to appreciate and enjoy it!

Then take some time to scrub your social media. Prospective employers are no longer ignorant to the many forms of social media their candidates engage in on a daily basis. Increasingly, Facebook, Twitter, LinkedIn, Instagram, and other forms of social media also serve as tools that employers use to screen candidates.

Usually media screening does not take place until you are a finalist or have been suggested for hire. When you have reached this place in the interview process, though, school and district administrators may look at your online persona to determine what it says about you and whether you are a fit with their culture.

A number of years ago, a colleague of mine interviewed a strong candidate for a specialized and difficult to fill position in her school. After the interviews were completed, the candidate was a shoo-in. The committee was extremely impressed and suggested that he be vetted by contacting references prior to hire. After leaving messages for the candidate's references, the principal had some time to kill, so she looked at the Facebook page of her top candidate. She was shocked to find that in addition to the usual pictures of family, friends, and various social engagements, he had posted photos of marijuana and other pro-drug images. This principal now had to consider whether a candidate willing to carelessly leave controversial images on his social media page would bring controversy to her school. Suddenly, her top candidate was beginning to look like a liability rather than an asset.

If you desire a professional position, it is time to scrub your social media. This is not to say that you can't still be you on Facebook, Twitter, Instagram, and other platforms. However, whenever you post a picture or comment, or when you link to another page or group, you need to ask yourself, "Do I want my prospective employer to see this?" If the answer is "No," then you would do well to remove it.

Another option, and one that I encourage regardless of how you choose to portray yourself online, is to use settings options to regulate who can and cannot view your online persona. Be careful, however, even if you use privacy settings. You might be surprised whom your prospective employer might know or with whom they might be "friends," potentially giving them access to your profile and postings. What you post and say online tells employers a lot about you. Make sure they like what they see!

Social Media as a Valuable Networking Tool

While social media is certainly a valuable tool for entertainment and communication, in recent years its use as a professional networking tool has grown exponentially. Now, professionals across the globe can connect and collaborate effectively and more efficiently than ever before. This being the case, I highly recommend that candidates in the education field consider the advantages of putting social media to work as a tool to increase exposure in the job market.

Twitter, for instance, has become my go-to for professional ideas and collaboration. No longer do I need to subscribe to professional journals and magazines to stay current on the latest trends in my field. All I have to do is follow my chosen educational innovators and I receive a real-time feed of their latest thoughts and efforts. And the best part is, they often follow you back!

This is a game changer for aspiring educators and those seeking new positions in their field. If you want to stay current on the needs of your desired school district or educational institution, like or follow them on social media. You will receive up to the minute updates on what is important to your prospective employer. This is only half of the advantage however. You can also use this platform to post the great things you are doing. Whether you currently hold a position in education or are completing your student teaching or internship experience, share what you are doing with the world! Perhaps you are trying some blended learning strategies or your students are taking on an authentic real-world project. Maybe you are attending a conference or professional development opportunity. Sharing your work and professional activities on social media lets people in your field know who you are and what you are about. Even sharing or retweeting a great article in your professional arena says something about you as a candidate who is a lifelong learner and stays current on the latest trends in their field.

There is a word of caution however. If you plan to use your social media presence for professional learning and networking, I would suggest that you use it for that purpose only. Getting decision makers in the field of education, counseling, etc. to follow you has numerous advantages. It can be a drawback, however, if you are also posting information about your personal life. If a friend tags you with something inappropriate or controversial or you experience some social media friendship drama, your followers are going to see that too. Remember, you are always being interviewed! Just as you would not share your deeply held political views at the interview table, you should not share them with your prospective employer on social media. For this reason, some professionals choose to maintain separate social media profiles for their professional and personal lives.

Care should be taken to maintain student privacy as well. Many schools ask parents to provide written consent to publish their child's likeness or work publicly. Not all parents choose to provide this consent. For this reason, you should be careful not to publish personally identifiable information in an effort to protect the privacy of your students.

By following a few simple guidelines, you can turn social media into a valuable self-marketing tool. Doing so will provide you with useful information about your prospective employer and may help you to stand out in the crowded world of education.

2

Interview Preparation

I've heard it said many times that there is no point in trying to prepare for an interview, because you don't know what the committee is going to ask. Nothing could be further from the truth. In his article about interviewing in a changing job market, Murty (2014) points out,

> ...a good number of candidates, despite having good academic background and track record, are not able to secure the jobs that they really want, for they are not able to handle the personal interview—the critical phase in the selection process—meaningfully and competently.
>
> (p. 51)

I would argue that time spent preparing for an interview has a value equal to solid gold. Police and military members train endlessly for a multitude of dangerous scenarios. They drill and drill and drill for the same crisis situations over and over again. Why? They do it so that when they are under the duress of actual battle or a real crisis situation, they will not be overcome by stress or fear, because their training will take over, making their response more automatic. The principle is the same when it comes to prepared interviewing.

The preparation I prescribe in these chapters allows you to enter the interview room with confidence. No matter what question is asked, you will be able to quickly and easily recall facts, ideas, and examples, because you have purposefully jogged your memory prior to the meeting. Better yet, you will be able to formulate your answers into coherent, concise responses, because you have prepared yourself to do so. The prepared interviewing techniques in this book make the difference between an interview being a nerve-wracking experience or a delightful conversation.

Stress Is Normal

Having conducted hundreds of interviews, I can say that approximately 80 percent of candidates are visibly nervous at some point, usually during the first five minutes. Employers know this. Nervousness is seldom a condemning factor. What they want to see is who can power through the nervousness to reach a point where they can represent their skills and abilities successfully.

David Rockawin (2012, p. 47) outlines four main types of anxiety that often tend to plague interviewees:

1. Fear of not having control of the situation
2. Fear of not achieving the desired outcome
3. Fear of being evaluated by others
4. Communication anxiety

The strategies described in Chapters 3 through 8 will teach you practical methods for reducing each of these fears. In this chapter, I will lay out a formula for successful interview preparation that will boost your confidence under stress and allow you to enter the interview session equipped with information and skills and ready for anything.

The goal of interview preparation is not to have canned answers for every question. If you approach your preparation this way, you will be caught off guard when the interview committee asks you a question for which you didn't think to prepare. Rather, the goal is to enter the interview session with your best accomplishments, awards, experiences, and philosophical viewpoints on the tip of your tongue.

Do you have a file cabinet in your home or office? If so, you likely access certain files often, perhaps weekly or even daily. If I asked you by name to locate one of these files, you would no doubt be able to walk to the cabinet, open the correct drawer on the first try, and pull the desired file in a matter of seconds. This is precisely the goal of inter- view preparation. Imagine your brain as a series of file folders located in drawers. The desired result of focused inter- view preparation is that, when asked any question, you will be able to quickly access the file in your brain that contains the desired information. When you are asked difficult questions, prepared interviewing will allow you to portray yourself to the committee as a wealth of experience and knowledge, because the information is fresh in your memory.

Imagine your brain as a series of file folders located in drawers. The desired result of focused interview preparation is that, when asked any question, you will be able to quickly access the file in your brain that contains the desired information.

When you are asked difficult questions, prepared interviewing will allow you to portray yourself to the committee as a wealth of experience and knowledge, because the information is fresh in your memory.

Know the Numbers

The field of education has become a data-driven environment. Therefore, I recommend wherever possible that you calculate statistics or factual numbers that quantify your previous successes. All of the candidates interviewed will, no doubt, state that they are the best person for the position. Employers are looking for concrete facts to back up your claims. For instance, rather than saying, "As an Algebra II teacher, I raised test scores for my students," look up the numbers and give a quantified statement, such as, "In my class, 93 percent of students passed the state exam, compared with 82 percent the year prior." Perhaps during your social work or counseling internship, you created a program to reduce behavior referrals. Crunch the numbers so you can say, "My behavior reinforcement program reduced office referrals by more than 20 percent." This strategy will serve you equally well when preparing your résumé, because quantified results always look better than vague generalizations about how effective your instructional strategies or philosophies might be.

Keep a File

A strategy that can save you time and effort is to keep an interview or job search file where you save records of your results and accomplishments. Whenever you crunch the numbers and see a success, record it on paper or in an electronic document and add it to the file. When you are given an award or nomination, add it to the file. Creating a running file of your successes will make updating your résumé a breeze and will ensure that you go into your interviews prepared with concrete, attention-getting data.

Maintaining a file is equally important as you progress in your education related career and desire to apply for new positions or leadership opportunities. Building an interview file throughout your career will save you valuable time and ensure your most relevant accomplishments and experiences are brought to light each time you interview.

The Big Five

The most high-yield strategy I can recommend for effective, pre-pared interviewing is knowing your Big Five. The Big Five are your five most important accomplishments or experiences that are relevant to the position for which you are applying. Think of these as the five important accomplishments or experiences you don't want to walk out of the interview without sharing.

Let's say, for example, that you are applying for a primary elementary teaching position. Before you even practice for the interview, sit down and determine your Big Five based on your personal work and experiential history. They might look some-thing like this.

1. In 2013, I received the XYZ award for outstanding undergraduate teaching from my university.

2. In 2013, while completing my student teaching, I parti-cipated in Professional Learning Communities (PLC) training (DuFour et al, 2016).

3. During my student teaching, 82 percent of students in my class scored proficient on the state assessment, up from 72 percent the year prior.

4. In 2014, I received training in Responsive Classroom strategies (see www.responsiveclassroom.org) for build-ing positive classroom community and have implemen-ted these strategies in my teaching.

5. In 2014, while working on my master's degree, I took part in a study to determine best practices for providing reading remediation to elementary students, and I have used these strategies in my classroom since.

When you have determined your Big Five, take time to unpack each of them. Jot down some notes for each one, indicating how you accomplished it and what philosophy or professional belief led you to organize or strategize this way. Imagine, for example, that you are an elementary teaching candidate, but you have no hired work experience. You have only recently completed your student teaching. Your Big Five, unpacked, might look something like this:

1. Each year, my university recognizes one student teacher for outstanding achievement in both the student's coursework and his or her practicum and student teaching experiences. I was chosen from more than one hundred candidates. The award was granted based on my overall GPA and my knowledge of innovative technology integration strategies that I used during my student teaching experience.

2. The school where I completed my student teaching was in the process of implementing PLCs building wide. I was able to attend trainings provided by the district. I practiced what I learned by participating in weekly PLC meetings with my teaching team throughout my student teaching experience.

3. I used benchmark test data, which I collected during the winter assessment period, to identify specific mathematics needs within my classroom. I used this information to form intervention groups based on individual student needs. My students improved by 10 percent on the state assessment compared with ratings the year before.

4. After completing my student teaching, I elected to take part in a full-day training in Responsive Classroom techniques. I have since used these strategies in my classroom, including daily morning meetings. I have found these strategies build strong community within the classroom and significantly reduce problem behaviors.

5. I was asked to take part in a yearlong research project testing the effectiveness of various early literacy strategies. The strategies I learned through this program include timed repeated readings and the use of close reading. These strategies have proven to be extremely effective in my current student-teaching classroom.

My Big Five Worksheet

Using this worksheet (or downloading a printable version from www.routledge.com/9780367189273), record your five most important job-related accomplishments, experiences, or honors that you want to be certain to share during the interview. Next to each, add a brief description to explain each achievement.

Accomplishment 1: _____

Description: _____

_____

_____

_____

Accomplishment 2: _____

Description: _____

_____

_____

_____

Accomplishment 3: _____

Description: _____

_____

_____

_____

Accomplishment 4: _____

Description: _____

_____

_____

_____

Accomplishment 5: _____

Description: _____

_____

_____

_____

The key here is to unpack each of your Big Five items and create a narrative or story that describes your success. Again, you are not creating a canned answer. Use the My Big Five Worksheet to help you develop your Big Five. The likelihood of your prospective employer asking you, "Please name your five greatest professional achievements," is not high. The goal here is to familiarize yourself deeply with the key aspects of your professional experience that make you a desirable candidate. This can be useful when you are asked interview questions like these:

♦ Tell me about a time you took the initiative to accomplish an important task without being formally asked.

♦ Describe a major project that you were responsible for and the degree of success your project experienced.

♦ Describe professional development you have received that has had a significant impact on your professional practice.

If you have listed and unpacked your accomplishments beforehand, when you hear such an interview question, your mind will immediately go to your Big Five. You will have a brief but detailed narrative describing exactly how you have met the desired need.

Interview Questions

Never before this present age have we had more information at our fingertips relating to any topic under the sun. This is of particular advantage to you as you prepare to interview. A simple Google search will yield hundreds of common interview questions. Often, with the right keywords, you can even locate likely questions specifically related

Never before this present age have we had more information at our fingertips relating to any topic under the sun. This is of particular advantage to you as you prepare to interview.

to your chosen grade level or area of educational expertise. Use this to your advantage! Create a bank of potential interview questions by cutting and pasting questions into a document you can save and return to easily.

Interviewers typically have thirty to forty-five minutes to learn as much as possible about candidates. They need to quickly see what you are like to determine whether your personality and social aptitude will be a fit for their school or district. They also need to figure out what you know, trainings or professional development you have received, experience you have teaching various grade levels or courses, and other helpful details. Finally, prospective employers need to know how well you can apply knowledge or how you would react if presented with typical situations common to the position. For this reason, interview questions typically fall into one of four categories:

1. **Introductory.** These questions focus on getting to know you. Introductory questions are often unrelated to a specific position. The employer's goal is to learn about you and possibly a little about your personality. These questions are also a great opportunity to demonstrate that you have effective social skills.

2. **Interpersonal Skills.** These questions focus on your ability to work and collaborate effectively with co-workers. Employers want to know if you can navigate tricky relational situations. They also want to know if you are going to cause drama through conflict or disagreements. In the educational field, these questions may also focus on your ability to establish a positive rapport with students or deal with difficult child behaviors. These questions can be a stumbling block for many candidates, so I encourage you to practice talking through these questions before the actual interview.

3. **Knowledge.** These questions are specific to the position for which you are applying. Prospective employers need to determine whether you have the knowledge, training, skills, and understanding necessary to do the

job. Here they are looking for relevant professional-development experiences or on-the-job training you have received.

4. **Application/Experience**. These questions ask you to apply your knowledge base to solve a hypothetical problem or to respond to a situation typical for the position desired. Here, it is essential that the candidate provide concrete examples of how they have handled a similar actual situation, if possible.

Some books or websites will offer hundreds of potential interview questions. Although these are certainly helpful, I find the sheer volume can be overwhelming and lead candidates to spend too much time trying to think of and practice every potential interview question. Remember, the goal of practice is to activate the file drawers of your mind so you can answer any question quickly and easily. For this reason, I have included fifty strategically chosen practice questions to get you started.

As you research questions, be sure to collect examples from each category. Aim for about twenty to thirty questions total. Again, the goal is not to try to practice answering every possible question. Even if you spent days gathering potential questions, I promise that when you are in the actual interview, your prospective employer will surprise you with a question you never thought would be asked. Rather than mastering answers to specific questions, the goal here is to familiarize yourself with the types of questions and subjects likely to be brought up.

Remember, you are refreshing the file drawers in your mind, so regardless of the question asked, you can quickly access your mental files for facts, experiences, and honors received that will allow you to answer any question intelligently and with real-life examples.

This is another place where networking can be used to your advantage. Use your connections or professional acquaintances to do some reconnaissance. For instance, if you are an aspiring

teacher, ask other teachers, your professors, supervisory teachers, or other colleagues to share questions they have been
asked before. If you hope to work as a school counselor, school
psychologist, or a paraprofessional, use your connections
within those fields to gather a bank of relevant questions and
topics. You can use these to develop a list of relevant training
and experiences. I will explain more about how to do this
efficiently and effectively in the next chapter.

It is important to note that even when you are fortunate
enough to be interviewed, you may not be hired. Knowing this,
make a practice of learning as much as you can from each
interview opportunity. After you leave the interview, return
home and jot down as many of the questions or topics as you
can remember. Save this list in your interview file. This way,
even if you don't get the job, you have gained experience and
know better how to prepare for your next interview.

Now that you know a little about the kinds of questions
you might be asked and the power of preparation, the next
chapter will focus on strategies for interview preparation.
A little time invested in practice before the interview can
make a world of difference for your confidence and effectiveness in the interview room!

50 Sample Interview Questions

Introductory or "Get to Know You" Questions

1. Tell us a little about yourself.

2. Describe your background. How has it prepared you for this position?

3. Why do you desire employment with our [school or district]?

4. Have you read any interesting books lately?

5. Finding balance between professional and personal life can be difficult. What do you do to reduce stress and ensure a healthy balance?

6. What do you like to do when you are not working?

7. What are your greatest strength and greatest area for growth?

8. Describe your teaching [counseling, coaching, professional, etc.] style.

9. What is your philosophy of education?

10. If I were to talk to some of your previous students, what would they tell me about you?

11. Imagine you are offered this position. What would you do after hanging up the phone? How about the next day or next month?

12. Describe a large-scale project you were responsible for. How did it go and what did you learn from the experience?

13. What steps do you take to organize your [calendar, lesson plans, educational data, meeting schedule, etc.] to ensure you meet professional deadlines?

14. Why should we hire you over the other candidates being considered?

Interpersonal Skills Questions

15. If I asked your supervisor or employer to describe you, what would he or she say?

16. Tell us about a conflict you experienced with a coworker. What steps did you take to address the concern?

17. How would you handle parents who have contacted you and are very upset about how you graded their child?

18. How do you build a rapport or "get along" with difficult students?

19. What steps do you take to motivate students who lack effort?

20. The district or school sets a mandate requiring you to change the way you do things and you don't agree. How do you proceed?

21. Teamwork is essential. What positive attributes would you bring to a team?

22. Describe your experience working in collaborative groups.

23. What steps do you take to ensure positive communication among colleagues or those under your supervision?

24. How do you handle conflicts or tricky relational situations at work?

25. When things become stressful, it can be difficult to remain positive. What strategies do you use to remain positive in negative situations?

Knowledge Questions

26. Tell us about a couple of professional books you have read lately. How have they had an impact on your work?

27. Describe your experience with [add name of curriculum used in desired district or school].

28. What would you bring to a teaching team to make it better?

29. Explain the difference between formative and summative assessment.

30. What does the term "diverse learners" mean to you?

31. Tell us about math interventions you have experience using in the classroom.

32. Tell us about reading interventions you have experience using in the classroom.

33. What training or experience do you have for meeting students' social and emotional needs?

34. What trainings or professional development opportunities have you taken part in recently?

35. You are in public and a colleague or parent begins to laugh about the embarrassing behavior of another student in your class. How do you respond?

Application/Experience Questions

36. How do you communicate with families about what is happening inside your classroom?

37. If I were to walk in to your classroom on an average day, what would I see or experience?

38. What steps do you take to differentiate instruction to meet the needs of all learners?

39. How do you use assessment results to inform your instruction?

40. What strategies or tricks do you use to determine whether your instruction is having the desired effect?

41. How do you ensure a culturally competent classroom that takes into account students' varying backgrounds?

42. Describe how you would meet the needs of struggling readers in your classroom.

43. Describe how you would meet the needs of students who are struggling in math.

44. How would you respond to a student who was repeatedly disruptive and refusing to comply with your requests?

45. What are the needs of twenty-first-century learners as you see them, and how would you go about meeting those needs?

46. What experience do you have using technology to create blended learning or flipped classroom opportunities?

47. Walk us through the process you use to plan lessons that incorporate essential state and/or local standards.

48. How do you go about celebrating individual or group success in your classroom?

49. A teacher approaches you about one student who is struggling in the area of reading. How would you go about diagnosing the concern and determining potential interventions?

50. How do you go about meeting the needs of gifted or accelerated learners?

3

Interview Practice
Example Sandwiches

Now that you have determined your big five and amassed a bank of potential questions on which to focus, it is time to practice. As I stated earlier, practice is what separates a polished interviewee from one who hesitates and struggles to put together a clear thought. I have seen hundreds of applicants stare at the ceiling, question after question, searching for what to say next. Don't let the interview be the first time you have organized your thoughts and reviewed your qualifications.

In this chapter, you will learn my proven methods for interview practice that will lead to confidence and success. Start by going through your compiled questions and writing notes under each to guide your answers. Some people like to write an actual essay answer for each question in paragraph form. Be careful if you do this, because you don't want to develop "canned" answers. For this reason, I recommend instead writing bullet points or outlining the answer. Use what works for you, though. The key is getting the essential information on paper so you can review it later.

Intension vs. Experience

In Chapter 2, we talked about the different kinds of questions you can expect from an interview committee. Many of these seek to uncover your prior experience in an effort to determine whether you know how to respond to various situations common to your chosen field. As you write your answers, be sure to include examples whenever possible.

Telling an employer how you would hypothetically handle a situation or respond to a need is one thing. Being able to share how you *have* handled a situation shows true grit and is what gets people hired. When creating your notes, always seek to include real examples from past experience to set you apart from the other candidates. Even if the experience was gained as part of a practicum or student teaching experience, you are better off to speak from a place of "This is what I have done," rather than "This is what I would do." Far and away, the greatest and most common mistake I see candidates make during the interview is failing to provide examples. Far too often, candidates provide clear and concise answers, but leave their answers grounded in the realm of the hypothetical.

> Being able to share how you *have* handled a situation shows true grit and is what gets people hired.

Let me explain my point with a brief story. A number of years ago, my wife and I took a single-engine plane trip to a remote fishing location in Alaska. As we waited by the plane for other passengers to load their things, I struck up a conversation with the youthful-looking pilot. "So, how long have you been doing this?" I asked. He quickly replied, "First time! But I've been practicing for a while now." My heart sank. I was about to embark on a single-engine plane flight through the bush of Alaska with a pilot who had not been adequately tested by experience. Soon a grin appeared on his face and he said, "I've been doing this for a few years now. I'm just messing with you." I'm sure my instant relief was obvious.

The truth is, experience always wins over intention. Employers want to know that you have been there and will know what to do in various situations. This being the case, examples of proven experience are, well, the *proof* that you've been there and know what to do. When used correctly, they frame the candidate as a proven and experienced professional. When neglected, they leave the candidate looking like a lot of talk and no action.

The truth is, experience always wins over intention. Employers want to know that you have been there and will know what to do in various situations.

Let's take a look at a very simple strategy to help you quickly formulate answers that don't just tell what you would do, but rather what you have actually done. Whenever possible, I encourage candidates to organize their verbal answers into a framework I have created to help them better understand this concept. It is called the Example Sandwich.

The Example Sandwich

My simple strategy, called the "Example Sandwich," helps candidates structure their answers in an interview. The Example Sandwich allows people being interviewed to craft an answer that positions one or more meaty examples right in the middle of their philosophy. Because the bulk of my professional work has been in the field of education, I have conducted hundreds of interviews for teaching, clerical, social work, and paraprofessional positions. One question I often ask candidates is "Describe how you would handle a student who consistently demonstrates disrespectful or inappropriate behavior." Often the answer goes something like this:

> I would try to talk to the student privately to determine what is causing him to be upset. I would explain my

expectations clearly and the consequences if he chooses not to follow the expectations. Finally, I would try to create an incentive for the child that would encourage him to focus on appropriate behaviors.

On the surface, this is a solid answer. It shows that the candidate balances clear expectations for student behavior with a proactive plan to deal with the root cause of the behavior. If you look closely, however, you will notice a theme. "I would," is repeated three times, signaling potential employers that this candidate has never actually done what he or she is describing. Unfortunately, it is an answer that is firmly grounded in the world of "what if." Because the candidate fails to provide an example, the committee is left to speculate on whether the candidate could actually implement the plan successfully should he or she be required to in real life. Let's look at another way to answer the same question:

Whenever I deal with chronic student behaviors, I believe it is important to balance clear, firm expectations with positive relationships and proactive measures. For example, during my student teaching experience, I had a student who was consistently defiant and disrespect-ful. Early on, I pulled the student aside privately and addressed the situation. I reviewed my classroom rules with the student and shared that I wanted her to be able to remain in my class rather than the office, but that I expected her to follow my directions and speak to me in a respectful tone at all times. Later on, I created a point sheet that allowed the student to earn a point for each day she was successful. I knew the student liked gui-tars, so when her point sheet was full, I allowed the student to earn thirty minutes of time playing my guitar during recess. Immediately, the student's behaviors began to turn around. The student knew what my expectations were, but she also knew I cared about her success and, in the end, this led to significant improve-ments in the child's behavior. This student is now a member of the school patrol, a position she earned in part due to her positive behavior change.

Now let's compare the second answer to the first. Which one leaves you feeling the candidate has a firm grasp on student behavior? The first candidate comes across as a person with good theories related to shaping positive behavior in students. The second candidate, however, by incorporating an anecdotal example, stands out as a proven and experienced practitioner. This second answer is structured using the Example Sandwich. Next, let's dissect this second answer to fully understand how the Example Sandwich works.

An Example Sandwich's Three Ingredients

The Example Sandwich, as I've developed it, has three parts:

1. First, share a core belief or philosophy that drives your work.

2. Next, provide an example from your practice to demonstrate your theory in successful action.

3. Lastly, close the answer by restating or summarizing how your core belief or philosophy yielded success.

Now let's label where these three components show up in the second candidate's answer.

1. **Belief/Philosophy:** "I believe it is important to balance clear, firm expectations with positive relationships and proactive measures."

2. **Successful Example:** "For example … I had a student who was consistently defiant and disrespectful. Early on, I pulled the student aside privately and addressed the situation … point sheet … playing my guitar …. Immediately, the student's behaviors began to turn around."

3. **Revisit Belief/Philosophy:** "The student knew what my expectations were, but she also knew I cared about her success and, in the end, this led to significant improvements in the child's behavior. ... [She's] now a member of the school safety patrol."

It is common for interview questions to include a statement such as "Please provide examples, if possible." More often than not, however, questions simply ask you to share what you know or what you would do. It is up to you as the interviewee to ensure that your answers demonstrate not only knowledge or philosophy, but proven experience as well. Let's look a little deeper at this concept by studying another example.

This question often shows up in educational interviews: "Describe how you use assessment results to drive instructional decisions."

Using the Example Sandwich, your answer might look something like this:

Belief/Philosophy: "I believe it is important to use both formative and summative assessment measures to inform my instructional practice. For this reason, I am constantly collecting ongoing informal assessments of student progress."

Example(s): "For example, when teaching math, I often end the period by having students complete an exit slip where they accomplish a problem that is representative of the day's learning. I look over these before the next class to determine whether I need to review any concepts before moving on to new material. Another method I often use is to review the learning target or goal at the end of the lesson and have students rate their progress toward the target on a three-point scale. I also use benchmark assessment data collected three times per year to determine whether students are making expected progress. I use the results from these assessments to drive my intervention groups, because they help me determine who is lacking number sense or place value understanding."

Revisit Belief/Philosophy: "I feel strongly that the constant, real-time feedback that ongoing formative and summative assessments provide are essential for being able to accurately diagnose the needs of my students."

Example Sandwich Worksheet

The Example Sandwich has three parts:

1. First, share a core belief or philosophy that drives your work.

2. Next, provide an example from your practice to demonstrate your theory in successful action.

3. Lastly, close the answer by restating or summarizing how your core belief yielded success.

Belief/Philosophy:_____

_____

_____

_____

_____

Example from Practice:_____

_____

_____

_____

_____

_____

_____

_____

_____

_____

_____

Restatement of Belief/Philosophy:_____

_____

_____

_____

These Example Sandwich Worksheets are also available in an 8 1/2 × 11 format that you can download from www.routledge.com/9780367189273. I suggest you use these worksheets as a template to develop and organize your notes for a few sample interview questions. You will not need to use the Example Sandwich to make notes for all of your practice questions in this way. When you get the hang of it, you will be able to use the Example Sandwich strategy right off the top of your head to answer any question.

It is important to note at this point that not all questions can or should be answered using this method. For instance, the Example Sandwich does not apply well when asked a question like, "Share your education and work experience that has helped to prepare you for this position." Answering this question by stating that you firmly believe in getting an education so you chose to go to college is not going to have the desired effect. There are some questions that simply ask for facts. Anytime you are asked to provide your work history, list your educational experiences or professional trainings, or provide dates or facts, simply answer the question. No need to make it harder than it is.

However, when you are asked to give examples or to explain how you would go about solving a problem or completing a task, it's time for the Example Sandwich!

4

Verbal Practice for the Interview

When you have finished collecting notes on potential interview topics and questions, written out your Big Five, and written out a few Example Sandwich answers you want to share, you are ready to begin verbally practicing your interview answers. I can't stress enough that your goal is not to create "canned" answers. I have completed interviews in which the candidates sounded as though they were reading their answers from a teleprompter. Answers like these are robotic and leave the interview committee feeling that you may not be confident about the topic, because you had to script your answers.

To avoid robotic or canned answers, the key is to practice answering the question naturally. It is okay to word your answers slightly differently each time. The idea is to include information from the bullet points that you included in your notes. Remember the Big Five mental file drawer we discussed? By verbally responding to questions, you are practicing going to the file drawers of your mind again and again. When you are asked a question during the interview, any question, this practice will allow you to access the mental file quickly and to provide a clear, concise, unscripted answer.

What I have found works for me personally is to begin by reading through my notes for a given topic or question. Then I try answering the question out loud. Yes, out loud. If this makes you feel weird, go someplace where you can be alone. Go to an empty room. Or park your car in a large parking lot—people will think you are on your phone using the hands-free feature! Just make sure you practice speaking through the answers verbally. This allows you to hear your own voice and decide if you like what you hear. Often I end up answering the same question multiple times, changing parts that I did not like until I get to a natural response I like. As I complete an answer, I review my notes briefly to see if I left out any of my important bullet points. If I have, I restate the answer again, making sure to add the critical information. It is important to note that I do *not* write my verbal answers out after I practice them. Doing so could lead to the canned or robotic answers you are trying to avoid. Remember, the goal of your practice is to create quick and easy retrieval of information.

Conduct a Mock Interview

After you have visited each of your questions or topics verbally, it is time to find someone to interview you. For me, it is usually my wife. On one occasion, when I was preparing for an interview that required a presentation, I even had my extended family members interview me almost like a panel. It is one thing to practice talking to yourself. It is another thing to speak to a live person.

A word of caution: When choosing a mock interviewer, the goal is not to be mocked! Choose someone whose advice you trust. We all have friends or family members who are good at giving us a bad time. These are not the people you want asking you questions and teasing

A word of caution: When choosing a mock interviewer, the goal is not to be mocked!

you about your answers. Select a partner who will be able to listen or who has the background and demeanor that will allow providing useful feedback.

The goal is to come out of this process confident, not self-conscious.

Right now, I can imagine what you are saying. "I don't want to be interviewed by my spouse, friend, or family member. That would be embarrassing." Let me ask you this, if you can't speak in front of a trusted friend or family member, how are you going to overcome your fear enough to speak clearly to a room full of strangers?

Mock interviewing has a number of positive benefits. First, research has suggested that the use of mock interview strategies is linked with improved interview performance (Rockawin, 2012). Another highly positive impact that practice interviews have is reducing interview anxiety by repeatedly putting candidates in an interview-like situation and allowing them to experience success under these circumstances (Rockawin, 2012).

Conducting a mock interview is not as hard as you think. Just hand your list of topics or questions to your chosen interviewer. Have the person randomly ask you questions rather than following your questions in order on the list. The actual interview will not be scripted to follow your order of questions, so hearing questions randomly is important.

As you are presented with questions, practice looking the interviewer in the eye while you provide your responses. Depending upon your personal comfort level with eye contact, this can be extremely easy, extremely difficult, or somewhere in between. Failing to look the interviewer in the eye or looking around the room as you answer is body language that suggests you lack confidence or are searching for what to say. The good news is that often during a real interview, the interviewer and the team will make eye contact primarily at the beginning of your answer. As you speak, they almost always look down to take notes. If you are able to provide answers to your practice partner(s) while maintaining eye contact for most of the answer, you will have no problem looking the interviewer or panel members in the eye during the real interview.

Again, do what works for you. I like to provide my interviewing partner with a handful of common introductory questions (see the 50 Sample Interview Questions) for which I have prepared and ask them to pick one of these randomly to start. Then I have them select other topics or questions from my list.

After I have answered approximately eight to ten questions, I stop for a short debriefing. I ask for feedback on my answers, but also on my body language and my pace. Don't be afraid to take some constructive feedback here. It is up to you to decide whether you will use the feedback or not, but it is better to consider changes or tweaks before the actual interview rather than during or after.

Interview Yourself!

If you don't have anyone to practice with or you are not comfortable practicing in front of a friend, fear not. There is an effective way around the need to have someone present to interview you: Interview yourself! Just find a quiet place, read yourself the questions and practice answering them. Consider using your smart phone, tablet, or computer to take video of yourself so you can go back and watch later.

Although most of us cringe at the thought of being recorded, doing so provides you with a great deal of insight and allows you to see yourself from the perspective of the interviewer. As you view your responses, pay attention to the rate of your speech. Do you tend to speed up your speech out of nervousness? Also pay attention to repeated words. Are you a person who tends to repeat certain words often? Or do you say "um" a lot? Finally, look at your nonverbal communication. Do you talk with your hands to the point of being distracting? Do you wring your hands or play with your tie when you are nervous? Taking time to view yourself will help you polish the nonverbal aspects of your interview, as well as the verbal replies.

It is important to note here that should you choose to record yourself, there is no need to collect video of all of your answers. Just record two to three responses. This will be more than sufficient to see how you present yourself. When you have had a chance to view a couple of responses, you can apply what you have learned to the rest of your practice.

As you practice, you may be tempted to work for hours trying to give the perfect answer. Most candidates do not need this much practice. It can, in fact, be detrimental to what you're trying to accomplish. Don't try to do too much at once. You are better off to practice in small amounts, perhaps fifteen to thirty minutes per day during a three- to five-day period, rather than to put in marathon practice sessions that can lead to fatigue and stress. You already did the bulk of the work when you wrote down your bulleted facts and information. If you don't have days to practice, put in an hour in the morning and perhaps another hour later in the evening on the day before your interview.

> **Don't try to do too much at once. You are better off to practice in small amounts, perhaps fifteen to thirty minutes per day during a three- to five-day period**

You don't need to log hours and hours of practice. Sometimes an interview comes up suddenly or unexpectedly. What if the interview is tomorrow and you don't have a lot of time? Look at it this way: Any thought or practice you do is positive and makes you better prepared. If you are short on time, focus on determining your Big Five and writing down your bulleted list of facts, accomplishments, and details you want to be able to remember. This process alone is extremely valuable and will help you make vital information easier to access mentally.

You can even spend time while driving to the interview talking through topics or potential questions. I have done this on more than one occasion. Your drive time, especially if you are a person who commutes to your current job or school, can be valuable practice time. Luckily, because we live in the age of hands-free cellphones, no one will look at you like you are nuts!

In review, whatever strategy you use, the importance of verbal practice cannot be understated. While mock interview experience is valuable, self-interviewing can be just as effective, especially for organizing your thoughts and experiences on a variety of interview topics. Use the Verbal Practice Strategies Checklist for the steps of good practice that I've included to help you get started.

Verbal Practice Strategies Checklist

❑ Start by generating a bank of practice interview questions.

❑ Write out your Big Five.

❑ Using your Big Five, take notes under each of your practice questions. Remember to keep your notes brief. Bullet-point lists or simple outlines work best.

❑ Provide real-life examples from past experience. Examples of what you have done always sound better than what you might do!

❑ On your own, read through your notes and practice answering questions out loud. Remember to answer appropriate questions using the Example Sandwich format.

❑ Give your practice questions to a trusted friend or family member to conduct a mock interview.

❑ Practice looking the interviewer in the eye, and monitor your speech for pace and volume.

❑ If you prefer, use your tablet or smartphone to video yourself and analyze the answers for content, pace, volume, and nonverbal tendencies.

❑ Relax! If you have followed the steps in this book, you will be more prepared than 90 percent of the other candidates who have not practiced.

Hit 2,000 Golf Balls a Day

I sometimes hear people say, "I don't want to practice my answers. I would rather keep it fresh and save it for the interview." To respond to this, I ask you to consider topics you love to talk about. For some it might be NFL football or other sporting events. Perhaps it is a favorite hobby or a political stance on a hot-button issue. If I randomly asked you to answer a question on one of your favorite topics, you would no doubt be able to do so with very little effort. You would probably be able to provide a number of facts to back up your opinions—and likely even do so with passion in your voice. Why? Because you have spent a great deal of time thinking about, reading about, and discussing these topics with co-workers at the water cooler or with friends on Friday night. The practice steps I am describing here are designed so that you can answer professional interview questions effortlessly and recall information easily, because you have thought about and talked about it before.

Let's face it. Interviewing is a stressful experience for most people. I have personally walked into interviews where I stammered out answers that lacked any depth and then walked to my car asking myself, "What just happened?" People who work in stressful jobs that require quick, correct decisions use repetition as their secret weapon. As I mentioned earlier, military personnel and police rehearse responding to stressful situations. They practice the same protocols and procedures again and again, so when a real crisis presents itself, they are able to respond automatically.

I once asked a professional golfer on the women's PGA tour how she became good enough to play golf for a living. What was her secret? She flatly replied, "Two-thousand golf balls a day." She then went on to tell me that she grew up at the local private golf club, spending her time at the driving range while her parents played the course. She would hit bucket after bucket after bucket of balls, practicing drives, short chipping, sand shots, and hitting around objects. This continued as she became a top high school player, college player, and later a pro.

When thousands of people are lined up on both sides of the fairway with their eyes on you, you can't be thinking about keeping your back straight, your head down, and following all the way through the ball. You need your response to be effortless, regardless of the shot that is presented to you, because it is automatic. You want it to feel comfortable, like you have been there before.

Practice speaking on likely interview topics prior to the date of your interview will allow you to feel much more calm and comfortable in the interview room. Practicing your answers is what allows you to be calm and to control your breathing during an interview. When the stress of the interview is in full force, it can be difficult to think straight. The relatively short amount of time you spend in practice allows you to respond to any question effortlessly, making you seem to the interview committee to be a well-spoken candidate with proven experience.

In short, practice allows you to present yourself as someone who has been there before.

In short, practice allows you to present yourself as someone who has been there before.

5

Difficult Questions
Made Easy

Most questions you will encounter in the interview will be pretty straightforward, but I have noticed a few that cause many people difficulty. No matter how seasoned you are in the interview room, questions about your weaknesses or those that ask you to describe how you handle conflict can be downright difficult to answer. This chapter will help you navigate tricky questions without missing a beat.

Greatest Strength and Greatest Weakness

One question just about everyone hates is the dreaded request, "Tell us your greatest strength and your greatest weakness." This question is just plain evil. I'm pretty sure it was designed by a disgruntled human resources genius to be impossible to answer without completely incriminating yourself! So what can a person do to avoid disaster when this bomb lands in your lap?

The interviewer's purpose with this question is to get a read on the candidate's limitations—but it is also an honesty check.

If you answer, "My weakness is I am just too productive and I will do anything to make my students successful," your prospective employer will laugh inside and know you are full of it. At the same time, you don't want to say something like "I'm not a morning person and I struggle with getting to work on time" or "I like to keep it real and say what is on my mind, even if sometimes people get offended by what I say." Answers such as these, though honest, will surely send up red flags with your potential employer. So how can you navigate a question like this without seeming to be either a liar or a potential dumpster fire for the school or organization?

The good news is there are ways to tiptoe through this minefield that will leave you in good standing with the interview committee.

Think of an area of your life that is a growth area common to most professionals. There are many of them to choose from. Perhaps it is being disinclined to say "No" and taking on too many projects at one time. Maybe you are a perfectionist, constantly striving to do better, and sometimes you need to accept a job well done rather than always reaching for a job perfectly done. We all deal with countless professional struggles, which your interviewers will be able to relate to as well. Choose one of these areas to focus on during your answer.

For instance, most of us struggle with balancing work demands and finding time to exercise, spend time with family, and similar priorities or activities. Don't tell the committee, "I struggle with balance." This will leave the impression that if they hire you, you are likely to burn white-hot for a while and then burn out. Instead, you could say something like this:

> An area that I have learned to keep in check is balancing professional and personal responsibilities. I am a very driven person at work and my tendency is to put in long hours. I find I am able to be more effective for my staff and more productive at work when I am doing a good job of taking care of myself outside of the school day. So that is an area I have learned to keep as a high priority.

When you say something like this, the entire committee is going to be thinking, "No kidding, that's totally me too! I'm always struggling to balance work with personal life!" By thinking of a common area for growth and describing yourself as being in a state of constant improvement in that area, you will avoid spilling your failures on the table. You will come off as a reflective professional who consistently focuses on self-improvement.

Interpersonal Conflict

Another line of questioning that can be difficult to navigate focuses on resolving interpersonal conflicts with co-workers. A question I often include in my interviews is "Tell us about a conflict you have had with a co-worker and how you resolved or didn't resolve the conflict."

Questions like these aim to give the committee a reading on how well you are able to relate to and collaborate with others. It doesn't matter where you work. If you work with people, there will eventually be conflict or disagreement in the workplace. Employers know this is unavoidable. So they are looking for candidates who can navigate conflict in a professional manner and work with colleagues to reach a common good that benefits the entire organization. What they want to avoid are rigid candidates who can't accept the ideas of others. They also want to avoid candidates who like to "stir the pot" and create drama in the workplace.

I have heard many answers to this question—not all of them good. I have heard candidates say, "I don't like conflict, so I just go along with what my co-worker wants, so I don't cause waves." This is not good, because it tells your prospective employer that you have no spine and can't stand up for yourself, even when you are right.

Others have said, "I marched right in there and set her straight. She never messed with me again." Yikes! Remember, you want to show you can *navigate* conflict, not nuke it!

Most often, candidates say, "I have never really had a conflict in the workplace. I just get along with everyone." Although this answer sounds strong on the surface, it may leave the committee thinking you are either not being honest or you avoid conflict at all costs. In answering this question and questions like it successfully, you want to give the impression that you have experienced natural conflict in the workplace (because we all have) and that you were able to communicate clearly and directly with the other person to reach a common ground.

So, how do we answer a question like this positively? Or when we have limited work experience? Let's look at some examples.

> you want to give the impression that you have experienced natural conflict in the work place (because we all have) and that you were able to communicate clearly and directly with the other person to reach a common ground.

Limited Experience with Work Conflict

Depending upon how long you have been in a school setting or professional position, it is certainly possible that you have not yet had to navigate a major conflict with a co-worker. You wouldn't be able to use an Example Sandwich in this situation. If this is the case, it is important to answer the question with examples of what you would do. Simply say something like,

> I can't think of a time I have had a conflict with a cow-orker. However, if I were to have a conflict, I believe it would be important to face the situation head on rather than waiting for the problem to fix itself. I would probably find a time to talk to the person privately. I would want to hear their side of the story to make sure I am considering all the information. At the same time, I would like to share my concern with them openly. By doing this, we increase the likelihood that we can land on a solution both parties can live with.

If you don't have an example from an educational setting, feel free to use one from your previous work experience or even a part-time summer job. The goal here is to demonstrate to the interviewer that you will handle conflict in a tactful, productive way.

Experienced with Work Conflict

First of all, when an interviewer asks, "How have you handled conflict at work?" it is okay to admit you have had a conflict with a coworker. The key is, try not to blame your former colleague for the conflict. The committee wants to hear you take responsibility for your actions, not condemn the actions of someone else. If you speak with condemnation, you will convince your prospective boss that once hired, you will do the same thing to her or him when things are not going well. You will also want to answer in a way that honors the confidentiality of your previous coworkers or clients. Candidates who have navigated this question effectively have typically said something like this (notice the Example Sandwich included):

A number of years ago, I had a disagreement with a colleague who provided service for special education students in my class. During parent–teacher conferences, parents of one of his students told me that they did not feel their child's IEP (individualized education plan) was being followed as written. Reviewing the student's iep, I noticed that the child was not receiving the service minutes required by the plan on a consistent basis. I believe in talking to people face to face when there is a conflict, rather than letting things fester and become worse. I scheduled a time to meet with my coworker and started the conversation by sharing how important their work is to our team and to our students. I then shared the feedback I had received from the parents and my concern that the child needed more support to match the iep. He felt bad and immediately shared some personal struggles he had been going through and owned up to not meeting with the student enough. We were able to come up with a plan to add in the additional time, and I was able to build rapport with my co-worker by being there to support him during a stressful time. Things were much better after that. As difficult as the conversation was, in the end, I felt we were a better team for the experience.

Notice how this answer follows the Example Sandwich approach? It includes a statement of philosophy (wanting to address concerns face to face) followed by detailed experience to back up the philosophy.

The response concludes by reviewing how use of this philosophical approach led to a desirable outcome for all involved.

By sharing a real example of conflict as well as evidence of how she successfully worked proactively to solve the problem, this candidate demonstrated that she should be able to solve future conflicts positively without bringing drama to the workplace.

6

The Day of the Interview

We have focused a lot on what to do to prepare before the interview. Now let's turn our gaze on what to do when your interview day finally arrives. (The Interview Countdown at the chapter's end summarizes a timeline to follow.) The day of the interview actually starts the night before. Make sure you get plenty of sleep and wake well-rested. Have a good, nutritious breakfast. If you have time and

> **The day of the interview actually starts the night before.**

it is part of your usual routine, be sure to get some exercise. Exercise and movement have been proven to stimulate brain activity and relieve stress. Both are perfect for your big day! The point is, take care of yourself. Do whatever necessary to be rested, healthy, and ready when it is time for your interview.

Dress the Part

I have seen people arrive at interviews in anything from a full suit to shorts and flip-flops. To answer the question, "How should I dress?" I go back to the work you put in getting to know your potential employer. Take a look around. What do those in your chosen organization wear? What is their dress code? Take notice of this in order to dress appropriately for your interview. A good rule of thumb is to dress a step up from the typical employee's regular attire. You can usually get away with overdressing a little, but appearing underdressed can be damaging.

Your dress says much to your prospective employer about your professionalism and preparation. Again, know the organization to which you are applying. In most cases, men should choose a dress shirt and tie and women should choose a professional blouse and slacks or skirt at a minimum.

If you are applying to a school, district, or university where formal dress is common, a suit is preferred. Avoid loud colors. The goal is for people to be dazzled by your interview, not distracted by your neon tie or blouse. Generally speaking, a suit in traditional navy blue, black or gray is the way to go. Choose ties, shirts, jewelry, or accessories tastefully.

Think of it like this. You don't want your dress to be particularly memorable or draw attention. You want your personality, professionalism, and experience, not your wardrobe, to be what stands out to the interview committee. Being remembered for your wardrobe happens when your dress is overly flashy, overly casual, or slovenly. Remember this is an interview, not a fashion show.

Take time to lay out your clothes the night before. Try them on to make sure they still fit and are clean. Many people don't wear dress attire or suits often. An hour before the interview is not the time to find out you have gained a few inches and your suit no longer fits. Iron your clothes and make sure there are no frayed areas, holes, or stains. I always check my tie carefully for stains. (Seriously, sometimes I think I need to wear a bib.) Consider getting your suit or dress clothing dry-cleaned as soon as you start applying for a new job. Do you have shoes fit for an interview? Are they comfortable and not something you will trip over? If not, it's time to run to the shoe store. Check your shoes for scuffs and if necessary polish them. In a nutshell, you want your dress to say, "I put thought and preparation into this meeting because it was important to me."

In a nutshell, you want your dress to say, "I put thought and preparation into this meeting because it was important to me."

Map Your Way to Success

Showing up late to your interview is almost a guaranteed interview fail. In the days before your interview, take a moment to search for the location online and get directions that include a roadmap. If you are using your phone to navigate, practice driving the route at the same time of day as the upcoming interview, so you can anticipate traffic flow or road construction. A GPS is not foolproof. Construction, map updates and the like can cause your phone or GPS device to lead you into trouble. More times than I can count, a candidate has arrived five minutes late to the interview saying, "Oh my gosh, I'm so sorry. I got completely lost" or "My phone led me to the wrong place." What the interview committee hears is "I didn't put enough thought or preparation into this to arrive on time." Do this and your prospective employer will, unfortunately, assume that you will approach important projects or clients the same way.

Think about the time of day and be mindful of traffic, bus routes, and train crossings. On one occasion I left an hour early for an interview that was thirty minutes away. I ended up getting stuck at a train crossing and my stomach turned when I realized that the train had applied its brakes! As the mile-long hulk of metal began slowing to a crawl, I was bouncing my knee and sweating with anxiety. Luckily, the train crept through the crossing leaving me just enough time to get to the interview on time and land the position. If I had said, "I'll leave forty-five minutes early and have plenty of time," I would have been late and likely would not have been hired.

It is also good practice to arrive early enough to run through a quick practice in the car. I often sit in the parking lot at the interview location for fifteen to twenty minutes before it is time to go in. I use the time to review my Big Five and glance over my notes or résumé so my past history and experiences are fresh in my mind. You are always better off to sit in the parking lot and have twenty-five minutes to review your notes than to rush nervously into your interview five minutes late.

Interview by Phone

Phone interviews are not extremely common, but they do take place, especially when the candidate is applying from out of state. If you are invited to this kind of interview, make sure you have prepared a space where you can take the call without interruption. When possible, try to be on a landline, or ensure you have a comfortable place to interview with stellar reception. Make sure you speak loudly and clearly enough so you can be understood. When doing a phone interview, you might consider emailing a photograph or video of your teaching to ensure the committee has a positive image in their head when they hear your voice.

Navigate Your Way Online

The same idea holds true for online interviews. In recent years, Skype, Google video calling, FaceTime, or other online, video-based interviews have become commonplace. Employers don't want to spend hundreds or even thousands of dollars to fly candidates out for face-to-face interviews, and they may lose candidates who are not willing to pay their own way. A more cost-effective method is to conduct the first round of interviews online. Although this is extremely practical, (and allows you to keep your pajama pants on), it can present its own ways of "getting lost."

Well before the interview, take time to experiment with the video platform that will be used. Make sure your computer or other device has enough memory and processing power to provide a clear video image without freezing or skipping. You may need to consider borrowing a laptop or desktop computer. Make sure you know how to identify and connect with the interviewer. If necessary, download the appropriate software. If you don't know how, ask a family member or friend. Or get help online: YouTube is full of tutorials that can help you with just about any video chat application. Think of it this way: Your ability to navigate the chosen video platform successfully is part of the interview.

Don't Sweat the Nervousness

One of the biggest concerns most people have with interviewing is the nervousness and anxiety that often accompany it. Following the preparation tips you've read in this book can go a long way to reducing and controlling nerves. That being said, I still get nervous during interviews. This is normal and, in many ways, expected by employers.

If interview nervousness is a struggle for you, I hope this will put you at ease: I estimate that 80 percent or more of the candidates that I interview show some outward form of nervousness during the interview session—whether shaky or clammy hands, a tremor in their voice, or talking too fast. Nerves and anxiety are common. The good news is that this is seldom a deal breaker. Relax! Employers know that candidates are nervous. In most cases, they have all been in your position and are empathetic to interviewees who seem nervous or tense. My personal tendency is to bomb the first question for no other reason than nerves. But after this, as I continue to interact with the interview team, I am able to settle into a groove and my preparation

> **Nerves and anxiety are common. The good news is that this is seldom a deal breaker. Relax!**

takes over. This is the key. Interviewers expect you to be nervous. What they are looking for is your ability to power through the nerves and provide a clear picture of yourself as a candidate. This is where your preparation pays off. When your mind is racing and your hands are shaking, the information you need will come to you, because you have prepared and the files of your mind are open and ready!

As an aside, one strategy I have learned that can help physically with nervousness is to take five calm deep breaths before the interview begins. Whether you are waiting in the reception area outside the conference room or have time to stop by the restroom first when you arrive, take thirty seconds to get some fresh air in your lungs. The added oxygen in your bloodstream will help clear your mind and can reduce many of the physical symptoms of anxiety.

Stay Positive

This next piece of advice may seem petty, but it involves an error that I have seen trip up interviewees more than any other issue. When answering questions, stay positive! I have heard candidates speak poorly of a previous coworker and admit they don't like certain software platforms. Throughout the interview, avoid negative comments about anything. Anything! Even commenting that you can't stand the recent cold weather can work against you. To prospective employers, candidates who complain or are negative in the interview are employees who complain at staff meetings, cause drama, and drag down morale.

> **When answering questions, stay positive!**

Sometimes, candidates don't realize that the object of their negativity is a school favorite, perhaps even a sacred cow. For all you know, a panel member knows and admires the person you insulted. Or maybe someone in the room has suggested the school use that software you said you hate to use. Perhaps the district has been devoted to a particular computer platform or brand for years.

Stop saying things like, "I hate the cold." Instead, say, "At least it is going to be a white Christmas." Turn, "I'm not a pc person," into, "Most of my experience has been with Mac, but I have worked with Windows and am confident that I can adapt quickly." Do this, and your prospective employer will see you as a flexible individual who can remain positive regardless of the circumstances.

Be Yourself

Allow me to offer one final thought about the interview itself that is essential. *Be yourself!* Employers want to find a highly qualified candidate with great skills, training, and experience, but they also want someone with a good personality. Sometimes in an effort to appear professional, candidates clam up and appear stiff or stoic. This does not give a good vibe to the interview panel. Often there are opportunities to laugh during the interview session, and when these come up, by all means, laugh! Be you. The interview is an opportunity for the organization to decide whether you are a fit, but it is also a chance for you to see if you will like working there. Don't pretend to be someone else. Smile, look people in the eye, and if invited to do so, don't miss opportunities to engage in small talk. Anything from, "I noticed your class ring. Did you attend xyz university?" to "Did you have a nice holiday weekend?" can be excellent opportunities to show them you are personable and fun to

> **The interview is an opportunity for the organization to decide whether you are a fit, but it is also a chance for you to see if you will like working there.**

be around. As an interviewer, I often chat up my candidates as I walk them down the hall to the conference room for the interview. This is purposeful. I want to know what the candidates are like when their guard is down.

Once I took part in an interview for a teaching position that involved placing a student in the office waiting area. The student's job was to strike up conversations with the teacher candidates as they waited. To the candidates, it looked like the student perhaps was in trouble and needed to see the principal or was waiting to be picked up by her parent. In reality, the student was part of the interview team.

After the interviews were over, we asked the student what her opinion was of each candidate. The information was extremely valuable! Some of the candidates took time to talk to the student and build rapport. Others ignored the student or were unwilling to participate in conversation. From this little experiment, we learned a lot about which candidates would quickly be able to establish positive rapport with students.

In short, trust yourself and be a real person. There is an old adage that you can teach a candidate the job, but you can't teach the person personality. Just be you and try to have some fun. The committee is not looking for the perfect professional. They want a real person who can be counted on to do the job well.

Interview Countdown

Six Months to a Year in Advance: Scrub your social media. Become a member of professional organizations in your career field. Takepart in conferences or professional development that is relevant to your field.

Three to Six Months in Advance: Begin researching the districts where you plan to apply. Search their websites, follow their administrators and superintendent on social media. Talk to people you know who work in the district.

Two Months in Advance: Identify your Big Five and create notes outlining the details related to your Big Five.

One Month in Advance: Compile a list of potential interview questions and start generating bulleted notes about each topic or question. No need to write essay answers. You are just creating file drawers in your mind so you will be able to remember your relevant knowledge and experiences later. Use the Big Five worksheet provided in this book to help you ensure you have examples to back up your philosophies!

One Week in Advance: Practice interviewing! Find a trusted friend or family member to interview you, so you can practice giving your responses. Use your smartphone to video record yourself. Practice answering potential interview questions while you are taking a walk or driving in your car. In your responses, practice using the Example Sandwich whenever it is appropriate.

A Couple Days in Advance: Map the route to your interview location and practice driving there during the same time of day as your interview. Keep an eye out for train crossings and construction, because these can mean significant delays! Try on the clothes you will wear to the interview. Make sure they fit and are clean and pressed.

The Night Before: Eat a good dinner and get a good night's rest.

The Day of the Interview: Relax! You have done your preparation. If you followed the suggestions in this book, you have likely prepared more than your competition. Remember to bring a notebook with your Big Five on the first page so you can refer to that information during the interview. Take some deep breaths, smile, and go get your job!

After the Interview: If you are not chosen for the position, send the principal a very brief but genuine note of thanks for the opportunity to have interviewed. If you were chosen, celebrate!

7

The Interview Itself and Follow-up

There is an age-old adage that says, "When in Rome, do as the Romans do." The point of this time-tested saying is that every culture has its own norms and expectations. The interview room is no different. In this chapter, I will walk you through everything from how to enter the interview room to how to wrap up the interview session with success. I'll even include some "interviewing don'ts" to help you avoid pitfalls of interviewing.

Arriving at the Interview Location

Through the years, I have noticed great variation in how early candidates arrive to the interview location. I have seen candidates arrive a full half-hour early or walk in seconds before their scheduled time. Plan to enter the interview site a little early, but at the same time not so early that the staff people wonder whether you forgot what time your interview starts.

Let's assume you arrived in the parking lot plenty early and have had some time to sit and review your notes before walking in. It is good practice to enter the building or office complex a little early—but *not* too early! Twenty-five minutes early is not respectful of the committee's schedule. If you arrive too early and the interview committee is running late (which they often are), you could end up sitting in the waiting room with the candidate who is to interview before you, which can be awkward and annoying.

Plan to enter the building and make your way to your interview location about ten minutes before your interview is scheduled to begin. Coming in at the last second, even if you are technically on time, suggests you barely made it. Ten minutes early indicates you are punctual and value timeliness.

Interviewing can be a long and grueling day for the interview committee. Although interviews can often run behind schedule, occasionally they may run ahead. If an interview ends early, committees will often check to see if the next person has arrived, so they can keep things rolling. If you are five to ten minutes early, not only will the committee notice you are punctual, but you may earn yourself a little extra time in the interview room if the interview is going well and the committee wants more time to get to know you. Remember that I mentioned you are always being interviewed?

> **Remember that I mentioned you are always being interviewed?**
>
> **This applies to waiting for your turn in the waiting room as well**

This applies to waiting for your turn in the waiting room as well. Being early gives you a little time to chat with the receptionist while you wait. If he or she is not conversational, don't push the issue, but my experience is that often the receptionist will ask you how you are doing or comment on the weather.

As a principal, I often make a point of coming out after the interviews are complete and asking the secretaries to share their impressions of the candidates. Don't think their opinion isn't important either.

Employers want to know not only whether you are qualified and can perform the essential duties of the job. They also want to know if you are personable and if coworkers will have an easy time communicating and collaborating with you. Show up at the last moment and you miss a golden opportunity to take part in this bonus interview!

Entering the Room

First impressions are everything so make your entrance count! The first minute of the interview, including the brief moments before you sit down to begin, are critical. Prospective employers will learn a great deal about your self-confidence, social skills, and personality before the first question is even asked. Stay calm and follow these simple suggestions for your interview to start off on the right foot.

> **First impressions are everything so make your entrance count! The first minute of the interview, including the brief moments before you sit down to begin, are critical.**

When someone is escorting you to the room, take a few slow, deep breaths while you are walking. As you enter, walk in with your shoulders back and a confident smile on your face. If you need to practice your posture in the mirror beforehand, do so!

One essential but easy component that many candidates forget is the handshake. If six people or fewer are in the room, it is good practice to approach and formally shake each person's hand. This shows respect and social competence, not to mention self-confidence. When you shake each person's hand, look them in the eye, grip their hand firmly and give it a good pump, while you say something like, "Nice to meet you" or "Thanks for having me." A limp grip and looking at the floor tells the team you lack confidence and perhaps social awareness as well.

Sometimes interview committees can be quite large, as many as twenty people or more. When this is the case, shaking each person's hand can take up valuable time. In this case, rather than shaking each person's hand, you can respect the committee's time and still show considerate social skills by making eye contact and offering a quick "Hi" or "Nice to meet you" to each of the team members as they are introduced. The key here is to enter with confidence and to engage positively with each member of the team.

Concluding the Interview

Most interviews conclude with an opportunity for the candidate to ask the employer any questions that he or she might have. In some cases, the employer will even ask the candidate if there is anything they would like to share that did not come up during the interview. For this reason, I encourage candidates to carry a notebook into the interview. If possible, class it up a little by using a business portfolio-style cover. On top of the first page of the notebook, list your Big Five. If you like, you can even add a few bullets under each of your Big Five items that provide details to jog your memory. Keep the notebook closed and to the side if possible. You can return to it at the end of the interview when asked if you have any questions.

I have personally used this many times in interviews to ensure that I have shared everything I wanted to before leaving. You may be concerned that having this information written down feels like cheating or the committee might not appreciate that you had to write it down.

The opposite is true. Having your key information prepared in advance demonstrates your high level of preparedness and suggests to the committee that you are thorough and complete in all you do.

On the bottom of the page or on a new page, write a few questions that you have for the employer. Generally, it is best to generate these questions in advance. If, however, something discussed during the interview brings a good question to mind, feel free to take a note to return to later. This is an important step, so don't take it lightly! Prospective employers learn a great deal about candidates by the questions they ask at the end of interviews. You want your questions to show that you are professional and care about your prospective employment being a good fit for all involved.

As mentioned in Chapter 1, a good time to develop questions is early on when you research the position. While you familiarize yourself with the school by looking at its website, jot down questions that come to mind. Good questions focus on curriculum, instruction, or the collaborative structure of the school. For instance, some good questions might look like, "Do you specialize in your upper elementary grades?" or "How often do your department teams meet in PLCs?" It is also common and acceptable to ask the potential employers for their timetable for making a decision.

Avoid asking questions about salary or benefits. These are great questions, but more appropriate to address after the interview when a position is being offered. The fact that many school districts now post their collective bargaining agreements, including updated salary schedules, on their district web pages means candidates can often know this information before interviewing. Check into that information on your own time. Finally, limit yourself to two or three questions. Employers appreciate a couple of thoughtful questions about the position or their school. Peppering the team with a laundry list of questions, however, is not respectful of the committee's time and suggests you lack social graces. In a nutshell, two or three thoughtful questions is the trick!

Finally, limit yourself to two or three questions. Employers appreciate a couple of thoughtful questions about the position or their school.

After the Interview

Following the interview, candidates often write me an email or send me a card thanking me for the opportunity. This is a nice gesture and generally will not hurt your chances of getting a job. Crafting such a follow-up demonstrates your professionalism and, especially if you are part of a multiple-interview process, can help to paint you in a positive light. Bear in mind, however, that this kind of follow-up message is likely to have little effect on the outcome. Few employers are going to say, "She wasn't my top choice, but then I got that nicely phrased thank-you email, and that changed everything!" For this reason, be brief and appreciative in your note. Whether you send a card or email, keep it simple. Here's an example:

> Thank you for the opportunity to interview with XYZ Middle School. I believe my strong instructional skills and my commitment to using data to guide my instruction would be an asset to your school district. If I can provide any further information, I can be reached at 555-5555. Thank you again, and I hope to hear from you soon!

Avoid trying to recreate your résumé in an effort to sway their decision. Employers are busy people and lengthy emails or letters can be seen as in convenient or even pushy. If you feel that you said something that garnered a positive response with the committee or that you have a specific skill that makes you stand out, it's okay to mention, but keep it brief. A simple statement will suffice, for example, "Thank you for the opportunity to interview with your team today. I believe my background using technology to create blended learning opportunities would be an asset to your school."

Being gracious in the face of defeat says a lot about a candidate's character. Even when you are not chosen for a position, sending a brief email or note to thank the employer for considering you can go a long way. If you were narrowly passed over in favor of another candidate, this can be an excellent way to ensure that you are brought back for an interview when another position becomes available. I have even heard of situations when a candidate was passed over, only to receive a call the next week and be offered a different position within the building for which the committee felt the person was a perfect fit.

The opposite is also true. I have had negative experiences calling candidates to deliver the bad news that they were not the one selected. Although most are very kind and thank me for the opportunity, from time to time others become noticeably upset, sigh deeply, or even question the decision, going so far as to ask why they were not selected. These responses are a good way to guarantee that you will not be called for future interviews. After you hang up the phone, then you can scream, pound the table, even throw your cellphone through a window if you like. While you're on the phone, though, stay professional. Remember that, as I mentioned earlier, people in hiring positions talk with one another. Burning a bridge with one organization is a good way to close doors with others as well. Also keep in mind that it is common for an employer to offer a position to the top candidate, who accepts, but then in the days after, the accepting candidate either gets cold feet or finds another position. Sometimes the chosen candidate is offered another job that offers more pay or is closer to the person's home. When this happens and the top candidate is no longer available, the runner-up will often get a phone call—that is, unless the runner-up showed his prospective employer a negative side when he was passed over.

> **After you hang up the phone, then you can scream, pound the table, even throw your cellphone through a window if you like. While you're on the phone, though, stay professional.**

Interviewing Don'ts

In summary, I would like to provide you with 10 Interviewing Don'ts that encapsulate much of what I've shared in this chapter. If you can avoid these simple pitfalls, you will do much to present yourself as your best self!

10 Interviewing Don'ts

1. **Don't go in blindly.**
    Take time to research your desired organization, its mission and ideals.

2. **Don't dress casually.**
    If you have to err, do so on the side of professional dress!

3. **Don't arrive late to the interview.**
    Being late says, "I lack responsibility and professionalism."

4. **Don't overlook the informal interview.**
    Be cordial with the secretary and those you meet in public.

5. **Don't forget to shake hands with your interviewers.**
    First impressions count! Show them you are confident and sociable.

6. **Don't forget to provide examples from your experience and achievements.**
    They want to hear what you have done, not what you might do.

7. **Don't get too long-winded.**
    Pay attention to how much time you have and adjust your answers accordingly.

8. **Don't speak negatively about anything or anyone.**
    You might be knocking someone they know or a program they are fond of.

9. **Don't let your social media undermine you.**
    Prospective employers will be looking at your online persona.

10. **Don't stress out!**
    Relax! Remember the interview is just a conversation, so be yourself!

8

Résumés, Cover Letters, and Applications

When I graduated from college as an eager, unemployed teacher candidate, I remember being told the importance of a good résumé. It was impressed upon me by my college advisor that the résumé could make or break my chances of getting hired and, therefore, should occupy a great deal of my time and focus. A lot has happened since then to change how employers screen candidates. The modern age of online application systems has streamlined how employers access application information. This, in turn, has affected how employers use résumés. In this chapter we will focus on the roles that the résumé and cover letter play in the hiring process, offer some helpful tips for writing these documents efficiently and effectively, and address applying online.

> **The modern age of online application systems has streamlined how employers access application information.**

The Résumé

In the modern age of online application systems and professional networking sites, the role of the résumé has changed
somewhat. The days of the paper and pencil application are all
but gone, even in the smallest school districts. Now, more often
than not, schools and districts use online application services.
In most of these, the résumé and cover letter are simply
scanned and loaded into the system, rather than mailed in
hard copy. The result is that the résumé does not play the
central role that it once did in educational hiring.

With new technology driving how we search for desired
candidates, the résumé is no longer the be-all-end-all of sum-
marized information. Think about it. Years ago when I first
started conducting candidate searches and screening candidates, I had to go to the district office and ask the human
resources clerk to give me the applications that had been
received for a given position. Then I spent hours physically
flipping through the pile, reading, taking notes, and, of course,
looking at résumés to find candidates with the experience and
skills we were looking for. In this kind of system, the résumé
was vital. It served as a one- or two-page synopsis of the
candidate's skills and experiences. In many ways, it was a
one-stop shop for applicant information.

Now all of this information, including the résumé, cover
letter, and application materials, is completed and uploaded
into the online application system by the candidate. With a few
clicks, principals and those in hiring positions can quickly
access the candidate's work history, educational background,
and licensure. Many online programs allow employers to
search the candidate pool according to desirable attributes. For
instance, if an employer wants to see candidates with reading
licensure, the employer simply clicks and the pool of two
hundred candidates is instantly narrowed down to the
seventy-five with the correct license.

Another problem that employers have with résumés is they
are typically unique in their format and layout. They even vary
greatly with regard to what kind of information is included. An

employer looking at résumés for work experience needs to quickly decipher each individual résumé to determine where this information is located.

With online application systems, employers no longer need to weed through countless résumés to find desired information. They can go to the online application and pull up the work history sections of each candidate in seconds. This allows them to view information about hundreds of candidates quickly and in one format. No longer do they need to decipher the résumé because the information is always in the exact same format for each and every candidate, saving the employer valuable time.

Focus on Your Online Application

So what does this mean with regard to your résumé? The take-away message is this: The résumé isn't the all-important document that it once was. This is not to say that you shouldn't have one or that it shouldn't be well written. It simply means that, although the résumé is still a required part of the application process, it does not necessarily receive the attention that the actual online application now does. Therefore, focus on making your application as clear and detailed as possible. This is where your prospective employer will be looking to learn the most about you.

Make Your Résumé's First Page Its Best

My advice regarding constructing your résumé is quite simple. Keep it short and to the point. In my experience, the average résumé receives at most a momentary read-through. The systems I have used to screen applications sometimes make the résumé part of the main profile screen the employer sees when looking at an individual application. You want the employer to be able to learn the most desirable information possible about you in the brief

> **My advice regarding constructing your résumé is quite simple. Keep it short and to the point.**

moments that their eyes scroll across it. For this reason, I suggest keeping your résumé to one page, two at the very most. If you are fresh out of a preparatory program, there is no reason to have a two-page résumé. If you have built up a wealth of experience and professional training, you may have to add a second page. If you do this, however, ensure that your best and most compelling information is on the first page. This is the page employers will likely see when your profile is selected or when they click to view your résumé. Information on the second page is likely to be missed because, let's face it, it simply won't be read!

Keep Your Résumé Clear and Simple

Avoid formatting information in paragraph form. Employers don't have time to read through paragraphs or even long sentences to search for information. Instead, provide clear headings such as "Work Experience" or "Education" and provide information in brief bullets. A sample résumé is provided next.

Sample Résumé

Anita Job

701 Quincy Street NW • Puckett, WA 44095

Mobile Phone (763) 555-5555

Email a.job@myserver.com

OBJECTIVE

To provide data-driven, results-oriented instruction to the students of Central Valley School District.

EDUCATION

May 2012   Gladden University   Glenwood, WA

Bachelor of Arts Degree in Education

- ◆ Noted areas of study included Educational Psychology, Special Needs and Multicultural field experiences.

TEACHING EXPERIENCE

2013-present Kent   Elementary School   Puckett, WA

Teacher, 3rd Grade

- ◆ Raised state mathematics test scores by over 25% in three-year period.
- ◆ Chaired committee to implement Professional Learning Communities.
- ◆ Led building-wide effort to adopt guided reading instruction.
- ◆ Served on the building technology committee tasked with implementing one-to-one handheld devices building-wide.
- ◆ Served on Puckett School District Standards-Based Report Card committee.

2012–2013   Glenwood Elementary School   Glenwood, WA

Student Teacher, 5th Grade

- ◆ Increased reading proficiency by over 50% according to spring benchmark tests.
- ◆ Served on the building technology committee tasked with implementing one-to-one handheld devices building-wide.
- ◆ Designed and implemented ten-minute fluency intervention, still in use by the school.

AWARDS AND RECOGNITIONS

Nominated for District Teacher of the Year, 2014–2015

Puckett School District Meritorious Service Award Nominee, 2013 Gladden Distinguished Undergraduate Teacher Award, 2012

One question that I sometimes hear from people creating their résumé is, "How do I get started?" The résumé is not the enigma many make it out to be. Microsoft Word has a number of templates that are simple and effective. You can use these templates to easily create a résumé that will get you into an interview. Also, I encourage you to show your résumé to colleagues or to your undergraduate or graduate advisor for feedback. There is no magic formula to writing a résumé. Don't make it harder than it needs to be!

The Cover Letter

This brings us to the cover letter. Cover letters, again, are a holdover from the days when human resources departments received hundreds of paper applications for multiple different jobs at the same time. The cover letter served as the candidate's way to declare for which job she was applying. It also gave the employer a brief example of the candidate's writing skills. Again, the modern age of applying for jobs has changed the landscape.

Employers no longer need to review cover letters to categorize applications by desired job. They simply log in to the application system, click on the desired position, and all of the applications for that job are at their fingertips.

I personally spend very little time looking at a candidate's cover letter. I give it a glance to get a quick feel for the candidate's writing skills, but then I move to the online application where the information I am looking for is laid out in a predictable manner and organized the same way for all candidates. Most online applications also have essay questions included. I can gain much more information about a candidate's writing abilities by reviewing these answers.

Keep Your Letter Short

The lesson to be learned is to put your time and thought into any essay or short-answer sections in the online application. Employers will read these sections and form opinions about you as a candidate. Brief answers that lack detail tell potential employers that you like to cut corners and avoid the hard work necessary to do a job completely.

Incomplete answers in these sections also rob you of a golden opportunity to share key information about what makes you the best candidate for the position.

Sample Cover Letter

March 25, 2016

Julie Stevenson
Washington Elementary School
800 West School Ave.
Alexandria, MN 56308

Dear Principal Stevenson,

I am writing this letter to apply for the 1.0 FTE Second Grade Teacher position currently open at Washington Elementary School. My experience as an elementary school teacher, as well as my diverse background in researching proven literacy interventions, makes me an ideal candidate for your school.

In my most recent position as a third-grade teacher, I raised state mathematics test scores by more than 25% in a three-year period. I also have been trained in and led staff in the implementation of Professional Learning Communities. In 2015, I was nominated for District Teacher of the Year for my efforts to guide a building-wide adoption of guided reading instruction.

With my strong background in literacy and experience with data-driven instruction, I believe I have a great deal to offer your school. I look forward to hearing from you regarding an interview. Please contact me on my mobile phone at (763) 555-5555 to schedule. Thank you for your consideration.

Sincerely,

Anita Job

Again, the "less is more" philosophy is the way to go when creating your cover letter. Try to keep the letter to one or two paragraphs. Simply state the position you desire and give a brief synopsis of your most desirable professional attributes. Use your Big Five to come up with these if needed. An example cover letter is provided on the previous page.

Edit Your Letter

Whether it is in your résumé or cover letter, one rule is key. Make sure your submission materials are error free. It is my belief that a résumé and cover letter alone will not land you a job, but they can prevent you from being interviewed for one if they are poorly written or if they contain spelling or grammatical errors. Errors in your résumé or cover letter suggest you lack attention to detail or that you simply lack grammatical understanding. Neither of these are desirable qualities in a new educator. Find a friend who is gifted in the rules of grammar and punctuation to read over your résumé or cover letter. Most colleges have a writing lab where people will help you edit your work. Bring your professional documents to them and ask for suggestions.

In short, don't overthink the résumé and cover letter. Create brief documents that highlight your best skills and attributes. Just make sure that what you create is clear and accurately written.

The Online Application

If the résumé isn't the be-all-end-all that it once was, then where should candidates put their focus? The answer is in the online application.

The online application is the résumé of today for those seeking a job in education. Put as much detail as possible in your online application because this is where principals and prospective employers will be spending the majority of their time learning about you. Again, be equally careful to ensure your application is free of spelling and grammatical errors before you submit it.

Provide Details

When writing the application, be complete. For instance, when sharing your work experience, share as much relevant information as possible.

> **When writing the application, be complete.**

Some systems allow you to share the location where you worked, previous salary, and dates of employment. Most, however, also allow you to provide a note about your experiences or activities completed while working there. This is a great place to share trainings, experiences, responsibilities, and honors that you received while in these positions.

As an example, don't just say you were a seventh-grade math teacher in XYZ School District. Use this space to make note of the fact that while you were there, you were the department chair, served on the Report Card Committee, or were nominated as teacher of the year for the district. If your networking has revealed to you any important information for which the employer is looking, such as experience working in professional learning communities (PLCs) or dedicated training to implement a specialized curriculum, make sure you share this in your work history.

Avoid leaving spaces blank within the application. Far too often I have read applications in which candidates left gaps in their employment or sections incomplete. A blank space sends a message to your prospective employer that you were in a hurry to complete the application and willing to cut corners. If you will do this in your application, they will assume you will do so in your professional work as well. If there is a space, fill it! Even if you have to write, "not applicable," that is better than a blank.

Prepare Essay Answers

Another area where less is *not* more is in the completion of essay questions. Most online application platforms allow employers to customize essay questions to fit a particular position. Give these questions careful consideration. When employers see briefly written, two- or three- sentence answers to application essay questions, they are left to assume the candidate lacks work ethic. If you are engaged in a task as important as seeking gainful employment and you won't spend the time necessary to write a thoughtful, clearly articulated essay answer, how can they have confidence you will put forth the time and effort necessary to create effective lesson plans or analyze student data?

Here again, ask friends or family members who are good writers to help edit your work. I encourage you to first write your answers in a Word or Google document. This way you can easily edit and later copy and paste them into the application when they are ready. This also allows you to keep your answers and save them for reference when completing future applications. Save these documents in your job file folder. One word of caution here. Some application programs do not format well when text is pasted into them. When this is the case, the application will often include a note that candidates should avoid pasting answers into them. If this happens, go ahead and type your answers directly into the application. Just be sure to copy them and paste the final version to another document before you submit, so you can save the answers in your job file. Many application systems will even allow you to print your final application when you submit.

> **ask friends or family members who are good writers to help edit your work.**

I encourage you to do this each time and file away your completed applications. This allows you to start a new application down the road without having to recreate the wheel each time!

Keep Information Current

Finally, update, update, update! Most online application systems now allow you as the candidate to maintain your profile or application in the system for a number of years. Sometimes candidates spend a year substitute teaching or filling in for a teacher in a long-term but temporary position before returning to the applicant pool the following year. All too often, when reading applications, I have noticed that candidates simply attach their existing application to new postings without updating the information inside to reflect recent work experience. Here again, you are always being interviewed! Submitting outdated information to prospective employers shows that you lack attention to detail and that you like to cut corners.

Navigating the application process, including the creation of a résumé and cover letter, does not need to be intimidating. Make your résumé brief—at least one page but not more than two. Make your most desirable information jump off the page. Similarly, by making your cover letter brief and focused on the right information, you increase the likelihood that it will be read. While brevity is the key with these documents, the opposite is true when completing the application. Focus on the application as the place to unpack the details of your candidacy—and you will increase your chances of giving your prospective employers what they are looking for in a candidate.

9

I Have a Job … So Now What?

So you have applied yourself to your college coursework, followed the guidelines prescribed in this book, and landed yourself the position you have been seeking. Congratulations! So now what? Is that all there is to it? First of all, celebrate! You have worked hard, stretched yourself, networked with others in the profession, and grown into a highly marketable educator. You deserve to celebrate your accomplishment. All of this being said, you may feel like you have reached your destination. The reality, however, is that being hired is just the beginning.

By the time you are hired into your first educational position, you have spent thousands of hours preparing for your chosen career. You have strived to excel not only in your coursework, but also in your practicum, clinical, and student teaching experiences. You have earned the recommendations of your college advisors and your supervising teachers. In short, you have invested an enormous amount of time, not to mention money, to get where you are.

While achieving your goal of being hired to a position in education is a major accomplishment to be celebrated, it is not all downhill from there. In most school districts, being hired marks the beginning of what is called the "probationary period" of employment. During this time, your new employer will determine whether you can deliver on what you promised during the interview and go on to become a consistent, positive force in the building. The probationary period is also a time for you to determine if your new position is a fit for you. In addition, budget cuts, changes in district programming, or other factors can have an impact on your ability to remain in your new position. This chapter will focus not just on how to keep your new job once you have it. Even better, it will show you how to flourish in your chosen position.

The Probationary Period

At the start of your new position working within a school district, there is typically a probationary period of approximately two to three years.

During this period of time, school districts evaluate the performance of their employees to determine whether the individual is a long-term fit for the organization. Think about it this way: Let's say you are about to purchase a new car. You know you are going to spend a great deal of money and the last thing you want to do is invest in a vehicle that will look good on the showroom floor, but will not perform as promised. This is why vehicle manufacturers include a warranty period of anywhere from three to ten years. Some even have a thirty-day period when you can return the car and receive equal value toward a different model. These features are great! They give you peace of mind knowing that if the car does not perform as promised or has structural or mechanical problems, you will not be tied to the responsibility of a substandard vehicle. Instead, you will be able to trade for a new vehicle without having to bear the long-term cost of a car that was not as advertised.

Hiring employees takes a great deal of time, effort, and money.

After the hire is complete, good employers will be committed to investing in the professional growth of their new staff members with ongoing mentoring and professional development opportunities.

Schools and districts want to hire and keep stellar employees for the long term, thereby ensuring the continuing quality of their organization. Naturally, school districts want to be certain that those they welcome in into their fold are employees who uphold their vision, values, and work ethic. In this way, the probationary period of employment serves as a proving ground, when the school or district gets to observe the staff member's performance over a period of time to determine whether what they saw in the interview aligns with what happens in day-to-day practice.

It is important to note that this period of time is also valuable for the employee. Although your new employer wants to measure your performance against your perceived abilities, it is just as important for you to "test-drive" your new district or organization to see whether it is a good fit for you. This is a time for you to experience life in your new school or district. During your first years in a new position, you will learn a great deal about the culture of the building in which you are working. You will experience the leadership style of your school's administrators and get a feel for the frequency and quality of professional growth opportunities your employer provides. In short, you also are test-driving the school or district to determine if it is a good place to spend your career.

Although your new employer wants to measure your performance against your perceived abilities, it is just as important for you to "test-drive" your new district or organization to see whether it is a good fit for you.

When you have obtained the position you seek, or better yet while deciding to which districts or organizations you would like to apply, it is a good idea to search the organization's website for information about the process for becoming a continuing contract or tenured employee.

Many school districts will post the master agreements for each of their bargaining groups to their website. These documents serve as an agreement between the organization and the staff members in each group as to the terms of contracted employment. These documents will contain valuable information not only about probationary status, but also the length of the contracted work day and year, holidays observed, payscale, and supplemental compensations the employee might receive. You are well served to spend time getting to know these contracts, so you can confidently enter into employment with the organization knowing that the terms of employment will be suitable to your needs.

During the probationary period of employment, you are likely to receive more frequent observation and formal evaluation than a tenured employee. This typically means approximately three formal observations during the school year, compared to perhaps one every two or three years for tenured staff. It will be important to shine during these performance appraisals, but this is only half the battle. Good principals know that anyone can put together a dog-and-pony show when they know their employer will be visiting. Principals are looking for teachers who are organized and prepared every single day. They want someone whom they know will provide standards-based, well-prepared instruction on a random Tuesday in the middle of January. You can show that you are this person by coming prepared every day, participating openly in professional development, and asking questions of more experienced staff members.

Anyone can have a bad day in the classroom—a day when nothing seems to work. We have all had those days when the technology fails, the copier eats your originals, and you feel like you need to scrape the kids off the ceiling to get them to their busses. Principals know there will be an ebb and flow to the school year and that no teacher is perfect. They are looking for teachers who are good, even on their "bad" days. By this I mean that even when things go wrong, the preparedness and professionalism of good educators allows them to see a tough day through.

Be a Lifelong Learner

So how do you survive the probationary period of employment? Are there any tricks for presenting yourself in a way that will help navigate the annual spring staffing process and ensure long-term employment?

In these situations, you might be tempted to think, "I'm just going to work my tail off for the first three or four years until I can lock up that tenured status. Then I can take my feet off the pedals and coast." I would caution readers to avoid this line of thinking. Presenting yourself as one professional personality for the purpose of ensuring long-term employment only to settle into a different, less growth-oriented person later on is unethical and a sure-fire way to frustrate your school's administration, colleagues, and team members.

The better answer is to focus on being a lifelong learner for the duration of your career. I hate to break it to you, but by choosing to pursue a career in education, you have chosen a field that is constantly changing. New research is always being conducted. New strategies are always being tested and developed, and technology is old almost as soon as it comes out. If you are not willing to apply yourself and grow throughout your career, education is going to frustrate you as a long-term profession.

> by choosing to pursue a career in education, you have chosen a field that is constantly changing

Think about it this way, in any other field or profession, would employers settle for employees who say, "I've learned enough. Leave me alone and let me do my thing the same way for the rest of my career?" Would any bank, business, or hospital allow its employees to say, "I'm not particularly invested in improving myself over time?"

When I was in the middle of my student teaching experience, I remember saying to my roommate, "I can't wait until I finish student teaching and get my first job. Then things won't be so busy and I can relax." When I graduated and found my first job, I enrolled myself in my master's degree program and thought, "I just need to push through the next couple years and then things will slow down." Soon after graduating with a master's degree in curriculum and instruction, I started to become interested in school leadership. My principal said he was willing to have me as a principal intern, and I was off to the races again, getting my administrative credential. Not long after receiving my certification, an opportunity presented itself to be an instructional coach. About this time I was having kids of my own, and soon I was an assistant principal. Then I got my first principal position. To stay relevant as a leader, I have had to read professional literature, participate in professional development, and various committees and work groups. So you are probably thinking, "What is he getting at?"

The point I am making is it never slows down. Sure, there are peaks and valleys in any career, but I have learned that those who are successful in education as teachers, counselors, social workers or paraprofessionals are those who are consistently committed, positive, and growth-oriented. When change comes, these people are not rattled. They find the gold nuggets in any learning opportunity and move forward more informed and more effective than before. They approach their craft as a distance race rather than a sprint. They are passionate about their work, but they also take time to invest in their families, their health, and their pursuit of outside interests.

These are the type of employees that employers look for and want to keep in their organization as long as they can. These people are a valuable asset to their school. They do amazing things for kids and ignite growth and positivity in others around them with the healthy professional example they present.

Commit yourself to being a lifelong learner. Each year in your career, choose one or two professional goals upon which to focus. Don't try to do it all at one time. Remember, this is a distance race. Set a healthy and positive pace for yourself and enjoy the journey!

Commit yourself to being a lifelong learner. Each year in your career, choose one or two professional goals upon which to focus.

The Annual Staffing Process

There are some aspects of your career you simply cannot control. Every year, schools and districts are affected by a variety of outside factors, such as changes in enrolment, financial restrictions, capital needs, and a fluctuating economy. At times buildings and districts simply are not able to keep employees, even when they want to very badly. This is all the more reason to become your best professional self early on in your career. My experience has been that "the cream always rises"—the strongest candidates typically seem to make their way to the top. If you are unfortunate to find yourself released from your contract during the probationary period for reasons beyond your control, having strong recommendations that speak of your highly successful performance will ensure that the hiring team members in another building or district will feel they have found a hidden gem when they review your application.

As a school administrator, I myself have been in this situation a number of times, having to let quality people go whom I would have much rather kept on my team. In these cases, I will often reach out to colleagues that I know are hiring for similar positions to let them know there is a diamond hidden in their candidate pool—someone they would be well-served to consider for an interview. Again, by committing yourself to long-term effort and growth in your career, you ensure success no matter what the circumstances.

Interviewing to Further Your Career

Getting hired does not mean that your interviewing days are over. As professional opportunities present themselves, it is highly likely that you will interview multiple times throughout your career. This being the case, the role prepared interviewing will play in shaping the success and direction of your career cannot be overstated. Simply put, what you bring to each interview can mean the difference between having a job and having the job you want.

Most of the people I know who have worked any significant period of time in education have worked in multiple positions and schools. You may choose to apply to a school or district closer to your home. Your chosen district may decide to add a district-level position that is right up your alley. You may decide to relocate your family for personal reasons or due to your spouse's career. In my own career, I have served as a classroom teacher, intervention teacher, instructional coach, assistant principal and principal. During my teaching career, I applied and interviewed for an opportunity to be a part of a team starting a new, project-based learning school for my district. Add it up, and you can see, you are likely to experience multiple interviews throughout your career. With so many crossroads in your professional pathway, should you leave the direction of your career to chance?

> **Most of the people I know who have worked any significant period of time in education have worked in multiple positions and schools.**

The preparation techniques presented in this book are designed to support you not only with landing your first job in education, but each desired position thereafter. As stated earlier, I highly recommend keeping a file of your successes, recognitions and awards. Doing so will make it easier to update your resume and complete the interview preparation described in this book. This book and the formula it contains are designed to be a companion that you can return to again and again throughout your career in education. My hope is that *Prepared Interviewing for Educators* will not only improve your interviewing, but help you experience a more fulfilling and satisfying career.

10

Closing Thoughts

During the course of this book, we've discussed sure-fire ways to improve your interview skills and deal with the stresses that accompany the interview process. We have even focused on what to do when you receive the job for which you are looking. You now have all of the tools you need to go out there and take hold of the job of your dreams. In closing, I would like to gift-wrap all that you've learned with a few final thoughts.

First, don't overdo it! The preparation in this book can and, if put to use, will make you a better interviewer. That being said, it is important that you not become consumed with preparation. If a theme runs through this entire book, it is that becoming rehearsed and robotic in your responses is not the desired goal. You also need to be careful not to create undue stress. Practice enough to make the file drawers of your mind easier to access and to make answers flow easier from your mouth. Then, stop! Take a break, relax, and trust your preparation. It may help to know that most of the candidates with whom you are competing are not preparing in a well-organized way. Trust yourself and the preparation work you are doing to bring you future career success.

A Note About Failure

Remember that the most successful professionals in history all had their share of failure and rejection. Carol Dweck (2006), in her game-changing book *Mindset,* shares cutting-edge research that proves it is not natural talent or ability that separates the most successful individuals from others. Rather, Dweck's work proves that successful people, whether in business, sports, or personal life, are those who use failure and setbacks as information upon which to grow and improve. *Mindset* is full of examples of individuals who experienced numerous rejections and used each of them to shape their lives toward breakthrough success.

Interviewing and getting passed over is *not* failure! As I stated earlier, there can be hundreds of applicants for a job, depending on the position. Know that getting an interview alone shows you have qualities for which employers are looking. When you are passed over after an interview, look at it as feedback! By interviewing, you get valuable practice and learn a little about what skills and qualities the employer wanted. Learn from this information and move forward with your head held high. On many occasions I have had to pass on an excellent candidate, because there was another candidate who just happened to be a perfect fit for the position in question. This is often how it goes. It also means that if you stay positive and keep putting yourself out there, you will find the right job, and then *you* will be the candidate who fits the position like a glove.

if you stay positive and keep putting yourself out there, you will find the right job, and then *you* will be the candidate who fits the position like a glove.

References

DuFour, R., DuFour, R., Eaker, R., Many, T. W., & Mattos, M. (2016). *Learning by doing: A handbook for professional learning communities at work* (3rd ed.). Bloomington, IN: Solution Tree Press.

Dweck, C. S. (2006). *Mindset: The new psychology of success.* New York, NY: Balletine Books.

Miller, D., Catt, S., & Slocombe, T. (2014). Job interviews: Keys for results. *Administrative Issues Journal: Education, Practice, and Research, 4(2),* 77–82.

Murty, G. R. K. (2014). Changed job market: The art of successfully navigating through job interviews. *The IUP Journal of Management Research, 13(3),* 50–67.

Rockawin, D. (2012). Using innovative technology to overcome job interview anxiety. *Australian Journal of Career Development, 12(2),* 46–52.

Made in the USA
Monee, IL
06 November 2019